MEXICAN MICROWAVE COOKERY

Revised

**A Collection of Mexican Recipes
Using the Microwave Oven**

by Carol Medina Maze

FISHER
BOOKS

Publishers: Bill Fisher
                  Helen Fisher
                  Howard Fisher

Editors: Joyce Bush
                  Helen Fisher

Art Director: Josh Young
Drawings: David Fischer
Book Production: Nancy Taylor

Published by Fisher Books
PO Box 38040
Tucson, Arizona 85740-8040
(602) 292-9080

Cover photos courtesy PACE® Picante Sauce.

**Library of Congress
Cataloging-in-Publication Data**
Maze, Carol Medina
    Mexican microwave cookery, a collection of Mexican recipes using the microwave oven/by Carol Medina Maze.
    —Rev.
    p.   cm.
    Includes index.
    ISBN 1-55561-039-0: $9.95
    1. Cookery, Mexican. 2. Microwave cookery. I Title.
TX716.M4M39   1990
641.5'882—dc20   90-46439
                                        CIP

©1990 Carol Maze

Printed in U.S.A.
Printing 10 9 8 7 6 5 4 3 2

Notice*: The information in this book is true and complete to the best of our knowledge. It is offered with no guarantees on the part of the author or Fisher Books. Author and publisher disclaim all liability in connection with the use of this book.*

Contents

Dedication

About the Author

Carol Medina Maze is a native of the Southwest, having grown up in Las Cruces, New Mexico. She has developed over 140 authentic, traditional recipes for the microwave oven. Many have been handed down through her family. Carol has blended her appreciation of native Mexican food with her professional training as a home economics teacher in developing and testing these recipes. She received her Bachelor's degree in home economics from New Mexico State University and her Master's degree in Education from Northern Arizona University. Carol resides in Phoenix, Arizona.

Acknowledgments

I thank my mother, Mary Louise Medina, for her invaluable contributions of traditional recipes. Some recipes are renditions of my great-aunt's, Guadalupe Medina. She established her culinary reputation cooking at ranches and inns in Southern New Mexico during the early 1900s.

Preface

This cookbook is for those who enjoy Mexican foods. Traditionally, Mexican foods took time to prepare and required the use of many pots and pans. With today's fast pace of living, one may not have time to spend in the kitchen. My book gives you a way to prepare Mexican dishes in about one-third the time. You save time, energy and effort, with fewer dishes and less cleanup. And you get this without sacrificing nutrition, appearance or flavor. Recipes in this book are from authentic and traditional Mexican dishes.

I always enjoyed preparing Mexican food, but I couldn't find Mexican recipes for the microwave oven. I began developing Mexican microwave recipes from old family recipes which I published in my father's Hispanic literature newsletter.

As I researched the Southwestern Mexican cuisine, I found many of the traditional recipes could be easily adapted. I compiled the recipes in a single cookbook, *Mexican Microwave Cookery*. I have now revised and added recipes in this book.

My culinary experience is based on my family life in the Mesilla Valley of New Mexico and on my training as a home economist. I am a 7th- and 8th-grade home-economics teacher. Since the publication of my first Mexican cookbook, I have presented cooking demonstrations before live audiences and on local and syndicated cable TV. My recipes have been reviewed in syndicated newspaper columns. My work has taken me to Northern New Mexico and Arizona where I learned about local customs involving Mexican cooking. My sister Agatha Rodriguez has lived in San Antonio, Odessa and El Paso, Texas. She has shared her knowledge about "Tex-Mex" cooking with me. I hope you enjoy cooking these recipes.

¡Salud y Buen Apetito!
To your health and good eating!

An Introduction to Mexican Cookery

Traditional Mexican foods are colorful with very distinctive flavors and aromas. The "special secret ingredients" which bring out the distinctive aroma and flavor include fresh or dried spices such as oregano, whole cominos (cumin), *azafrán* (Mexican saffron), garlic, fresh or dried cilantro (coriander), onion, bell pepper, chiles, tomatoes and *tomatillos* (small green Mexican tomatoes).

Mexican foods, with their complementary spices, provide important nutritional benefits. Fruits, grains (corn, wheat and rice) and vegetables, including legumes (primarily beans and peas), provide high fiber. Beans are a good source of vegetable protein and contain no sodium or fat. Spices and herbs offset the need for salt. Many of my recipes emphasize the use of high-fiber, low-cholesterol ingredients without a lot of salt.

Traditionally, Mexican foods are cooked slowly to enhance the distinctive flavors of the chiles and spices. In microwave cooking, the flavors and aroma of the chiles and spices are equally preserved. All recipes in this cookbook have been developed and tested in the microwave oven. They are categorized into various dishes or *comidas*. For example, dishes which contain corn or flour are referred to as *comidas de masa*. Recipes containing chicken are referred to as *comidas de pollo*.

Recipes provide information on power levels, cooking time and number of servings as well as the ingredients, method of preparation and nutritional analysis.

The Microwave Oven

The microwave oven is convenient and saves time. Once the microwave oven is turned on, microwaves are emitted within the oven cavity. The microwaves pass through nonmetallic materials such as glass, ceramic, paper and plastics and thus penetrate and cook food. Microwaves are reflected by metal materials and will not cook food contained in metal dishes. Use appropriate microwave cookware.

Microwaves cook from the outside toward the inside so many foods may need to be stirred during the cooking time because they cook faster on the outside. Also, rotating dishes when cooking helps to ensure uniform cooking.

Some microwave ovens do not have variable heat settings. They cook at 100% power; heat is controlled only by the length of cooking time.

The following table shows equivalent heat settings for different makes and models of most microwave ovens. For example, if a recipe calls for 70-percent power, that is equivalent to a heat-select setting of 7, a cooking level of medium-high power, a fractional power level of 2/3 and a temperature level of roast. Heat created from microwave energy continues to cook

foods after microwaves have penetrated them. Some microwave recipes call for a "standing time." This is when heat in the food itself continues cooking after the microwave cooking time.

EQUIVALENT SETTINGS

Percent Power	Heat Setting	Cooking Level	Power Level	Temperature
100	10	high	full	high
90	9	*	*	sauté
80	8	*	*	bake/reheat
70	7	medium-high	2/3	roast
60	6	*	*	simmer
50	5	medium	1/2	defrost high
40	4	*	*	defrost low
30	3	medium-low	1/3	soften
20	2	*	*	warm
10	1	low	1/10	low
0	0	*	*	rest

* No available setting—must adjust cooking time to nearest setting on microwave.

Some microwave ovens have variable power settings, others cook only on high power. If your microwave oven only cooks on high power, you will have to adjust cooking times for power settings in these recipes. For example, a dish cooked with a power level of 50%

(medium) 20 minutes would be cooked on 100% (high) 10 minutes.

Different microwave ovens require different cooking times due to atmospheric conditions, elevation and electric power. It is important to know the wattage of your microwave oven. Recipes in this book were prepared in a 650-watt oven that boiled 1 cup of tepid water (78F, 25C) in an average time of 2 minutes and 46 seconds at 1300 feet elevation.

If your oven operates at a different wattage or boiling time, you may need to adjust cooking times accordingly. A label on your oven specifies the wattage. To determine boiling time, measure 1 cup of tepid water (78F, 25C). Heat the water on 100% (high) until bubbles begin to break.

Tips and Facts on Microwave Cooking

Recipes in this cookbook require various types of coverings for the cooking dish. If the recipe says to microwave without mention of covering the dish, leave the dish uncovered during cooking. When the recipe says "cover with waxed paper," completely cover the dish with a piece of waxed paper before microwaving. The same applies for recipes calling for lids or plastic covering. If the recipe says "cover and microwave," a microwave-safe lid, waxed paper, plastic wrap or a paper towel can be used.

Both density and moisture content of the food make a difference in cooking time. Moist foods cook faster. Foods with a thicker consistency or a greater mass take longer to cook.

If your microwave oven does not have a shelf, place a casserole on top of an inverted bowl. This allows microwaves to penetrate evenly around the dish and ensures more uniform cooking. Stirring, rearranging foods and rotating dishes also help.

Microwave Cookware

A variety of cookware is safe to use in the microwave oven. The following dishes are used to prepare the recipes in this cookbook:

casserole dishes (1-1/2 quart, 2 quart, 2-1/2 quart, 3 quart and for candy recipes, 5 quart); flat-bottom casserole dishes or glass pans (8 x 8 inch and 12 x 8 inch); glass measuring cups (2 cup and 2 quart); browning dish; glass pie plate; and glass loaf pan (8 x 4 x 2 inch).

The browning dish has a special coating on the bottom. When the dish is preheated, it will brown foods such as tortillas and fajitas. Other flat-bottom dishes are not designed for browning foods in the microwave oven. Although I recommend preheating a browning dish 4 to 5 minutes, follow the manufacturer's directions for preheating your dish.

Caution: Use hot pads or oven mitts when handling a preheated browning dish.

The microwave pressure cooker is helpful for preparing stew, bean and meat recipes. Several microwave pressure-cooker recipes are included. Before using a pressure cooker, read and understand the manufacturer's instructions.

Warning: Do not use a regular pressure cooker designed for stove-top cooking. When removing a microwave pressure cooker from your microwave, use oven mitts or hot pads to protect your hands. The pressure cooker gets hot!

Some recipes call for a microwave-safe ring mold. If you do not have one, you can create one by inverting a custard cup in the center of a round, glass cake dish or shallow casserole. The ring shape allows recipes such as meat loaf to cook evenly.

If you plan to make microwave candy, you may want to buy a microwave-safe candy thermometer. Don't use your regular candy, meat or oven thermometers because they won't work in the microwave. Stores specializing in microwave ovens and accessories sell thermometers for microwave use.

Ingredients and Substitutions

Ingredients called for in these recipes are readily available at most supermarkets. If not available, a substitution may be used. Following is a list of ingredients and some substitutions.

❧ Anise seeds
Substitute liquid anise or licorice flavoring.

❧ Azafrán (Mexican saffron)
Substitute turmeric to achieve the yellow color; however, the flavor of azafrán cannot be duplicated.

❧ Chiles (fresh green chile)
Use canned green chiles.

❧ Cilantro, fresh (coriander)
This spice is also called *Chinese parsley*. There is really no substitute for this spice except perhaps dried coriander leaves. Use one half the quantity called for in the recipe.

❧ Cilantro seeds (coriander seeds)
Although there is no substitute for coriander seeds, powdered coriander can be used. The flavor of coriander seeds is different from that of fresh coriander leaves.

❧ Cominos, whole (cumin)
Substitute powdered cumin for whole cominos.

❧ Masa harina
A corn-flour mixture used primarily to make tortillas and tamales. Corn meal is not a substitute for masa harina.

❧ Mexican chocolate
For 1 ounce Mexican chocolate, combine 1 ounce semi-sweet chocolate (one square), 2 teaspoons sugar, 1/8 teaspoon vanilla and 1/8 teaspoon ground cinnamon.

❧ Oregano (fresh or dried)
Substitute ground oregano for fresh or dried.

❧ Piloncillo (Mexican brown sugar shaped in a cone)
Piloncillo is also called *Panocha*. Dark-brown sugar can be substituted in the same quantity.

❧ Tomatillos
These small green tomatoes have paper-like husks. If unavailable fresh, you may find them canned

and referred to as *tomatillo entero* or *tomate verde*. Small green tomatoes (of the garden variety) can be substituted though the flavor will not be equivalent.

❦ Vegetable Shortening and Oil

Vegetable shortening and vegetable oil can be substituted for lard, bacon drippings or butter in traditional Mexican recipes. I use canola cooking oil. In many of my recipes I use a non-stick vegetable cooking spray for preparing the cooking dish instead of oiling.

Hints and Tips

The following hints will help reduce fat and salt while conserving the flavors of Mexican food.

Select lean cuts of meat (beef and pork). Trim all excess fat. Remove fat and skin from poultry (chicken and turkey); much of the fat is in or attached to the skin.

Microwaving allows you to reduce the amount of cooking oil needed to sauté. If you would rather eliminate the use of cooking oil to sauté, try using defatted, low-sodium beef or chicken broth. Chill homemade broth and remove solidified fat from the surface.

Substituting 2 egg whites for each whole egg lowers the fat and cholesterol in a recipe.

Use a reduced-fat cheese, or cheese made from skim milk. Some choices include reduced-fat cheddar, Monterey Jack and mozzarella.

Use lard-free flour tortillas made from low-saturated-fat vegetable shortening. Coat tortillas with vegetable oil or water when softening or shaping them.

In recipes calling for whole milk, half-and-half or cream, substitute a combination of nonfat dry powdered milk and skim milk.

Documentation:

Nutrient analysis was calculated using *The Food Processor II*, version 3.0, by ESHA Research. Analysis does not include optional ingredients. Only the first choice ingredient is calculated. The higher number is used for the range in servings. Abbreviations are: **Cal** = Calories; **Prot** = Protein; **Carb** = Carbohydrates; **Fib** = Fiber; **Tot. Fat** = Total Fat; **Sat. Fat** = Saturated Fat; **Chol** = Cholesterol.

Chiles y Salsas

The Rio Grande River Valley of Southern New Mexico is known as the Mesilla Valley. The farmlands of this valley are ideal for growing the long, broad green chile known throughout the Southwest. The rich irrigated fields and the cool night air that flows into the valley from the nearby San Andreas and Organ Mountains make for ideal growing conditions. Come mid-July, people from Las Cruces go to the farms to pick and buy their fresh green chiles. I remember that every summer my mother would bring home a burlap bag of chiles which I was delegated to assist in roasting.

I can recall the aroma of freshly roasted green chiles that would fill the air in the late summer months in Las Cruces. My mother and the neighbors would roast the chiles either in their kitchens, using a cast-iron skillet, or outside on their barbecue grills, if large quantities were being roasted. This practice evolved from the method used by my great-grandmother at the turn of the century. In that time, a pit was dug and filled with mesquite wood. The chiles were then roasted on a grill over the glowing mesquite charcoal. This later became a practice of roasting chiles on a wood stove during my grandmother's time. From pit to wood stove to barbecue grill, the transition has accelerated the cooking process but the tradition of chile and its flavor has more or less remained the same.

The red chile can equal the green chile in unique flavor and aroma. The red chile is simply a green chile that has ripened on the vine or has been picked when mature and sun dried. The mature fresh red chile has a sweeter taste and has a higher concentration of vitamin A than the dried red chile. When the chile has ripened to a red color, it can be picked and roasted in the same manner as a green chile. Roasted, mature red chiles can be used to make red-chile rellenos, enchiladas, salsas and fresh red-chile soup. Dried red chile is used to make salsas, Chile Colorado and various red-chile meat dishes.

The season of the red chile in the Mesilla Valley is as culturally significant as football and *Diez y Seis de Septiembre,* the 16th of September, one of Mexico's two independence days. From mid-September to the first frost, the chile fields change from green to brilliant red. It was, and still is, a common practice for people to pick and string mature red chiles by the stems into "ristras de chile." You can drive the rural roads of the valley and see the huge strings of vivid red chiles hanging from the porch rafters and walls of the adobe houses. The chiles are also picked to sun dry in the farmyards and on roof tops. The landscape is dotted with brilliant red patches of chiles drying in an autumn scene.

When I was four or five, my mother would send me to my great-aunt Lupe to help at her neighborhood variety store. She would prepare the family chile in a *cedazo* or cone-shape colander, which at the time seemed very big.

She would mash the softened chile pods with a red-chile-stained wooden pestle. The red pulp would ooze through the colander and collect in a big blue enamel pot. She would warn me that chile burns and would display her reddened hands. She then washed her hands with mild soap and warm water and rinsed in a bowl of white vinegar to relieve the burning.

For those who do not care to make their own salsa, I recommend PACE® Picante Sauce.

Roasted Green Chiles

It's really easy!

Power level: medium-high
Cooking time: 14 minutes
Servings: 6 chiles

6 fresh green chiles

Vegetable oil

Fresh chiles should be either the Anaheim chile, referred to as the California or long green variety, or the New Mexico chile de ristra ancho chile, a full broad variety. Prepare green chiles by this microwave method or a conventional oven-roasting method.

Caution: Chiles can irritate your hands and eyes, particularly if the chile is hot! I recommend that you wear rubber gloves when roasting, peeling and scraping chiles. Avoid touching any facial area when handling chiles. After handling chiles, wash your hands thoroughly with soap and water.

Rub each chile pod with oil; pierce each pod on both sides with a knife so steam will vent. Place chiles in a flat-bottom casserole. Cover with waxed paper; microwave on 70% (medium-high) 7 minutes. Turn each chile; rotate dish.

Cover and microwave on 70% (medium-high) 7 more minutes. Chiles will not brown or blister. Wrap chiles in a damp cloth; let stand to cool. This helps to separate the skin from the flesh. Remove pods from damp cloth; peel under cool running tap water.

Each chile contains:

Cal	Prot	Carb	Fib	Tot. Fat	Sat. Fat	Chol	Sodium
18	1g	4g	1g	0	0	0	3mg

Pico de Gallo

Rooster's Beak

A spicy fruit salsa. Perhaps this dish is called Rooster's Beak *because the custom of eating chunks of fruit with the forefinger and thumb depicts a rooster "pecking."*

Power level: high
Cooking time: 4 minutes
Servings: 4 cups

1 lb. (about 2 cups) jícama, peeled, cut into cubes

1 (11-oz.) can mandarin oranges, drained, reserve 1/2 cup liquid

1 cup fresh pineapple chunks or 1 (8-oz.) can unsweetened pineapple chunks, drained

Pomegranate seeds from 1 pomegranate, if desired

2 tablespoons sugar

1/2 teaspoon crushed red-chile pepper

1 tablespoon chopped fresh cilantro

1 tablespoon lime juice

Combine cubed jícama, mandarin oranges, pineapple chunks and pomegranate seeds, if desired, in a 1-1/4 quart bowl and set aside.

To make sauce, put 1/2 cup reserved mandarin-orange juice into 1-quart bowl, add sugar, crushed red chile pepper and chopped cilantro. Stir. Microwave on 100% (high) 4 minutes, stirring after 2 minutes. Cool in refrigerator 15 minutes. Add lime juice and pour over fruit; combine. Chill at least 30 minutes before serving.

Each tablespoon contains:

Cal	Prot	Carb	Fib	Tot. Fat	Sat Fat	Chol	Sodium
9	0	2g	0	0	0	0	1mg

❦ **Variation**
Other fruits can be substituted. Try fresh oranges or grapefruit sections, apples, papaya, mangoes or pears.

Cousin to the sweet potato, jícama is a brown, turnip-shaped vegetable. Its white interior tastes like a water chestnut. Use as an accompaniment to salads.

Blanched Tomatillos

For authentic flavor in green sauces, use tomatillos.

Power level: high
Cooking time: 4 minutes
Servings: about 1 cup

8 tomatillos

Remove husks, the outer paper-like skins. Cut each tomatillo in half; place in a glass dish. Cover with waxed paper; microwave on 100% (high) 4 minutes, rearranging tomatillos after 2 minutes.

Remove skin from tomatillos; chop remaining pulp. If removing skin is difficult, scrape pulp from skin with a spoon.

Each tablespoon contains:

Cal	Prot	Carb	Fib	Tot. Fat	Sat Fat	Chol	Sodium
13	1g	3g	1g	0	0	0	6mg

Literally translated, tomatillo means "little tomato." Although a tomatillo is a fruit, as are all tomatoes, it is treated as a vegetable. The husk of a tomatillo turns from green to tan as it ripens. Use the tomatillo while the husk is green; once the husk turns tan, the tomatillo may be overripe. When purchasing tomatillos, pick the ones that are enclosed by a husk.

Salsa de Cominos

Cumin Dip

A "lite" dip that can be used for tortilla chips, salads or as a topping for fajitas, machaca or tostadas.

Servings: 1/2 cup

1/4 cup dairy sour cream

1/4 cup plain yogurt

1/4 teaspoon cumin powder

1/4 teaspoon red-chile powder

1 tablespoon chopped onion, if desired

1 tablespoon red bell pepper, if desired

Put all ingredients, except onion and bell pepper, in blender and blend until well puréed. Add onion and bell pepper, if desired. Stir well. Refrigerate until ready to serve.

Each tablespoon contains:

Cal	Prot	Carb	Fib	Tot. Fat	Sat. Fat	Chol	Sodium
20	1g	1g	0	2g	1g	3mg	10mg

Make your own sour cream by combining 1/4 cup cottage cheese, 2 tablespoons lowfat milk and 1 teaspoon lemon juice in a blender and blend until well puréed. Makes about 1/4 cup. Refrigerate until ready to serve.

Salsa de Piña

Pineapple Salsa

Attractive-looking, it makes a great accompaniment with any type of meat or fish dish. The "sweet hotness" is a great taste.

Power level: medium-high
Cooking time: 6 minutes
Servings: 1 cup

1 cup finely chopped fresh pineapple or 1 (8-oz.) can unsweetened pineapple chunks, drained and finely chopped

1 tablespoon sugar

2 tablespoons finely chopped onion

1 tablespoon finely chopped jalapeño chile

1 tablespoon red bell pepper, if desired

Put all ingredients in a small bowl, stir. Cover with waxed paper and microwave on 70% (medium-high) 6 minutes, stirring after 3 minutes. Allow to cool and serve. If a finer texture is desired, put cooked Salsa de Piña through food processor.

Each tablespoon contains:

Cal	Prot	Carb	Fib	Tot. Fat	Sat. Fat	Chol	Sodium
8	0	2g	0	0	0	0	8mg

Taco-Seasoning Mix

Use this instead of a 1-1/4-ounce package of commercial taco-seasoning mix.

Servings: 3 tablespoons

1 tablespoon red-chile powder

1/2 teaspoon salt

1 teaspoon garlic powder

2 teaspoons onion powder

1 teaspoon paprika

1 teaspoon cumin powder

1 teaspoon ground oregano

1 teaspoon sugar

Combine all ingredients in a small bowl until well blended. Store in an airtight container for future use.

Each tablespoon contains:

Cal	Prot	Carb	Fib	Tot. Fat	Sat. Fat	Chol	Sodium
26	1g	6g	1g	1g	0	0	383mg

My favorite condiment for Mexican main dishes is this spicy seasoning mix. I make quadruple amounts and store some for later use. Paprika gives a rustic color when the seasoning mix is added to a dish cooked in the microwave.

Taco Sauce

Everyone's favorite sauce with tacos or other Mexican specialties.

Servings: 1 cup

1 (8-oz.) can stewed tomatoes

**1 cup chopped green chiles or
1 (7-oz.) can diced green chiles**

1 garlic clove, mashed

1/4 teaspoon dried-leaf oregano

Salt to taste

Chop stewed tomatoes and combine all ingredients until well blended. Place in an airtight container. Refrigerate sauce up to 7 days.

Each tablespoon contains:

Cal	Prot	Carb	Fib	Tot. Fat	Sat. Fat	Chol	Sodium
7	0	2g	0	0	0	0	24mg

Chile Colorado

Red Chile Sauce

Excellent for tamales, chile meat and other dishes.

Power level: medium-high
Cooking time: 15 minutes
Servings: 3-1/2 cups

20 dried red-chile pods, stems and seeds removed

1/4 teaspoon cilantro seeds

1/4 teaspoon whole cominos

1 teaspoon dried-leaf oregano

1 garlic clove, cut in half

1/4 cup coarsely chopped onion

1/2 teaspoon salt

3 cups warm water

Place all ingredients in a blender; process until puréed. Place mixture in a 2-quart casserole. Cover and microwave on 70% (medium-high) 15 minutes, stirring after 7 minutes.

Each tablespoon contains:

Cal	Prot	Carb	Fib	Tot. Fat	Sat. Fat	Chol	Sodium
7	0	2g	0	0	0	0	20mg

Some recipes in this book use Chile Colorado uncooked. This means it is not necessary to cook the puréed mixture before adding to the other recipe.

If dried red-chile pods are unavailable, substitute 1/2 cup pure red-chile powder and 1 tablespoon all-purpose flour. Place chile powder, flour and all remaining ingredients in a blender; process until smooth.

Salsa Ranchera

Ranch-style Sauce

Try it on eggs or other Mexican dishes.

Power level: high, medium
Cooking time: 8 minutes
Servings: about 3-1/2 cups

2 cups chopped green chiles or 2 (7-oz.) cans diced green chiles

1 (16-oz.) can stewed tomatoes

1 cup chopped onion

1 garlic clove, chopped

1 teaspoon dried-leaf oregano, crushed

1/2 teaspoon salt

1/4 teaspoon whole cominos, crushed

1/4 teaspoon cilantro seeds, crushed

Combine all ingredients in a glass bowl. Cover with waxed paper; microwave on 100% (high) 3 minutes or until mixture begins to boil.

Reduce microwave setting to 50% (medium); continue cooking 5 minutes. Serve sauce hot or cold. Refrigerate up to 7 days or freeze until ready to use.

Each tablespoon contains:

Cal	Prot	Carb	Fib	Tot. Fat	Sat. Fat	Chol	Sodium
5	0	1g	0	0	0	0	33mg

🌶 Variation
For added spice use jalapeño chiles.

Molcajete y Tejolete

A *molcajete,* pronounced mohl-kah-heh-teh, and *tejolete,* pronounced te-ho-leh-teh, is a three-legged mortar and pestle made of volcanic rock. It is used for grinding spices and making chile sauces. Using this device can save time, although it is not absolutely required for grinding and mashing. In many of my recipes I use the term "crushed" with cilantro and comino seeds. Crushed seeds can be made by grinding the seeds in the molcajete. Seeds can also be crushed by using a fork, although they are ground to a finer texture in the molcajete.

Salsa para Enchiladas Verdes

Green-chile Enchilada Sauce

Excellent for green-chile tamales as well as enchiladas.

Power level: high, medium-high
Cooking time: 7 minutes
Servings: 2 cups

1 tablespoon vegetable oil

1 garlic clove, mashed

**1 cup chopped green chiles or
   1 (7-oz.) can diced green chiles**

2 tablespoons all-purpose flour

1/2 teaspoon cumin

1 cup water

Salt to taste

Combine oil and garlic in a 1-1/2-quart casserole. Cover with waxed paper; microwave on 100% (high) 2 minutes. Stir in remaining ingredients. Cover with waxed paper; microwave on 70% (medium-high) 5 minutes. Cool before serving.

Each tablespoon contains:

Cal	Prot	Carb	Fib	Tot. Fat	Sat. Fat	Chol	Sodium
8	0	1g	0	0	0	0	0

Salsa de Legumbres

Vegetable Dip

Looks like Guacamole Dip. Tastes great!

Power level: high
Cooking time: 1 minute
Servings: 1-1/2 cups

1 (16-oz.) can cut green beans, drained

1 (8-1/2-oz.) can sweet peas, drained

1 cup chopped tomatoes

2 tablespoons chopped onion

1/4 cup chopped green chiles or 1 (4-oz.) can diced green chiles

1/4 teaspoon cumin seeds, crushed

1/4 teaspoon dried-leaf oregano, crushed

1 teaspoon vegetable oil

1 teaspoon lime juice

Salt to taste

Purée beans and peas in a food processor or blender. Set aside.

Put tomatoes, onion, green chiles, crushed cumin seeds, oregano and oil into a 1-1/2 quart casserole dish. Microwave on 100% (high) 1 minute.

Add puréed beans, peas and lime juice to vegetables and blend well. Salt to taste. Refrigerate at least 30 minutes before serving. Serve in place of guacamole dip.

Each tablespoon contains:

Cal	Prot	Carb	Fib	Tot. Fat	Sat. Fat	Chol	Sodium
15	1g	3g	1g	0	0	0	70mg

Salsa de Tomatillo

Green-Tomato Sauce

Serve this colorful sauce on tacos and flautas.

Power level: high
Cooking time: 2 minutes
Servings: about 1-1/2 cups

1 tablespoon vegetable oil

1/4 cup chopped onion

1/2 teaspoon cilantro seeds, crushed

1 garlic clove, mashed

1 lb. fresh tomatillos, blanched, page 5

1/4 cup chopped green chiles or 1 (4-oz.) can diced green chiles

Salt to taste

Combine oil, onion, cilantro and garlic in a 1-1/2-quart casserole. Cover with waxed paper; microwave on 100% (high) 2 minutes. Stir in tomatillos and chiles. Add salt to taste. Refrigerate until ready to serve.

Each tablespoon contains:

Cal	Prot	Carb	Fib	Tot. Fat	Sat. Fat	Chol	Sodium
11	0	1g	0	1g	0	0	2mg

Chile Barbecue Sauce

Top any meat or poultry dish with this spicy sauce.

Power level: medium-high
Cooking time: 20 minutes
Servings: 1-1/2 cups

3 tablespoons Taco Seasoning Mix, page 8, or 1 (1-1/4-oz.) pkg. taco seasoning mix

1 tablespoon red-chile powder

1/4 cup tomato paste

1 tablespoon Worcestershire sauce

2 tablespoons brown sugar

1 teaspoon dry mustard

2 tablespoons vinegar

1 tablespoon vegetable oil

1 cup water

Combine all ingredients in a glass bowl. Cover with waxed paper; microwave on 70% (medium-high) 20 minutes, stirring after 10 minutes. Refrigerate until ready to use.

Each tablespoon contains:

Cal	Prot	Carb	Fib	Tot. Fat	Sat. Fat	Chol	Sodium
17	0	3g	0	1g	0	0	82mg

Mole Colorado

Red Chile Sauce

The unusual combination of red chile, chocolate, cinnamon and peanut butter gives this Mexican sauce a unique taste. This is the famous sauce used for chicken or turkey mole.

Power level: medium-high
Cooking time: 30 minutes
Servings: 3-1/2 cups

3 cups chicken broth or beef broth

1 (8-oz.) can tomato sauce

3 tablespoons Taco-Seasoning Mix, page 8, or 1 (1-1/4-oz.) pkg. taco seasoning mix

2 tablespoons red-chile powder

1/3 cup creamy peanut butter

1/3 cup unsweetened powdered cocoa

2 tablespoons sugar

3/4 teaspoon ground cinnamon

Combine ingredients in a 2-1/2-quart bowl. Cover with waxed paper; microwave on 70% (medium-high) 30 minutes, stirring every 10 minutes. Use at once or refrigerate until needed.

Each tablespoon contains:

Cal	Prot	Carb	Fib	Tot. Fat	Sat. Fat	Chol	Sodium
27	1g	4g	1g	1g	0	0	39mg

❦ Variation

Power level: medium-high
Cooking time: 15 minutes
Servings: 4

Place 3 cups cooked, shredded chicken or turkey into a 2-1/2-quart casserole. Pour 2-1/2 cups Mole Colorado over chicken or turkey. Cover with waxed paper and microwave on 70% (medium-high) 15 minutes, stirring after 7 minutes. Serve hot.

Mole Verde

Green Chile Sauce

*Another delicious sauce for
seasoning chicken or pork.*

Power level: medium-high
Cooking time: 15 minutes
Servings: 3 cups

**1/2 lb. tomatillos, blanched,
    page 5**

1 or 2 jalapeño chiles

2 cups chicken or beef broth

1/2 cup coarsely chopped onion

1/8 teaspoon coriander seeds

**2 tablespoons fresh coriander
    or parsley**

1 garlic clove

1/4 teaspoon whole cominos

1/4 cup chopped walnuts

1/2 cup chopped almonds

1/4 teaspoon salt

Cut blanched tomatillos in half.
Place all ingredients in a blender
or food processor; process until
puréed. Pour sauce in a 2-1/2
quart bowl.

Cover with waxed paper; microwave on 70% (medium-high) 15
minutes, stirring after 7 minutes.
Refrigerate until ready to use or
freeze up to 2 months for later use.

Each tablespoon contains:

Cal	Prot	Carb	Fib	Tot. Fat	Sat. Fat	Chol	Sodium
16	1g	1g	0	1g	0	0	12mg

Mole originated with the early
Aztecs. Mole is a sauce made
with chile, nuts, tomatoes or
tomatillos and spices. Many
moles are prepared with chocolate and cinnamon. Mole can
be used as a sauce for turkey,
chicken or shredded pork.

Chile con Queso

Chile with Cheese

A creamy chile-cheese sauce, great for dipping tortilla chips.

Power level: high
Cooking time: 5 to 6 minutes
Servings: 2 cups

1 tablespoon vegetable oil

1/2 cup finely chopped onion

1 garlic clove, chopped

1/8 teaspoon whole cominos, crushed

1/4 cup chopped green chiles or 1 (4-oz.) can diced green chiles

1-1/2 cups diced processed cheese (12 oz.)

1/2 cup evaporated skimmed milk

Combine oil, onion, garlic and cominos in a 1-1/2-quart casserole. Cover with waxed paper; microwave on 100% (high) 2 to 3 minutes or until onion is transparent.

Add chiles, cheese and evaporated milk; stir to blend. Cover with waxed paper; microwave on 100% (high) 3 minutes, stirring after 1-1/2 minutes or until cheese melts. Serve hot as a dip or sauce. Mixture can be frozen for later use.

Each tablespoon contains:

Cal	Prot	Carb	Fib	Tot. Fat	Sat. Fat	Chol	Sodium
48	3g	1g	0	4g	2g	10mg	157mg

Chiles Rellenos

Baked Stuffed Chiles

Long, wide green chiles work best for this recipe. Chiles Rellenos can be stuffed with cooked ground beef, turkey, tuna, shrimp or refried beans.

Power level: high
Cooking time: 5 to 6 minutes
Servings: 3

6 whole roasted chiles, page 3, or 1 (7-oz.) can whole green chiles

1 cup shredded Cheddar cheese (4 oz.)

3 eggs, separated, or 4 egg whites

1/4 teaspoon cream of tartar

2 tablespoons all-purpose flour

1/2 teaspoon baking powder

1/8 teaspoon salt

1/8 teaspoon pepper

1/4 teaspoon paprika

1 tablespoon vegetable oil

Cut a lengthwise slit in each chile; remove seeds. Leave stem on. Fill each chile with cheese, reserving 1/2 cup cheese for topping. In a small bowl, beat egg whites until stiff, gradually add cream of tartar.

If using egg yolks, combine in a separate bowl. Add the egg yolks to the flour, baking powder, salt, pepper and paprika; beat well. Fold flour mixture into egg whites. Pour batter into a shallow glass dish.

Spread oil in a 12" x 8" casserole. Dip chiles in egg batter; place chiles in casserole. Microwave on 100% (high) 2 minutes. Turn chiles over. Microwave on 100% (high) 1 to 2 minutes or until batter is set. Top chiles with reserved cheese; microwave on 100% (high) 45 seconds or until cheese melts.

Each serving of 2 chiles contains:

Cal	Prot	Carb	Fib	Tot. Fat	Sat. Fat	Chol	Sodium
323	18g	14g	2g	22g	10g	253mg	445mg

Chile y Queso al Horno

Chile & Cheese Bake

Combining chiles and cheese gives this dish a great taste.

Power level: high
Cooking time: 4 minutes
Servings: 4

1/2 cup green-chile strips

3/4 cup shredded Cheddar cheese (3 oz.)

2 eggs or 3 egg whites

1/2 cup skim milk

1/4 cup nonfat dry milk powder

1/4 teaspoon paprika

3/4 cup fresh bread crumbs

1 tablespoon margarine

1-1/2 slices of wheat bread make approximately 3/4 cup bread crumbs.

Grease or spray with a vegetable cooking spray a 1-1/2-quart casserole. Using half the chile strips, make a layer of chiles in casserole. Top with half the cheese; set aside.

Beat eggs in a separate bowl; add milk, dry milk powder and paprika. Beat mixture well. Pour egg mixture over chiles and cheese. Top egg mixture with remaining chile strips.

Place bread crumbs in a bowl; cut margarine into bread crumbs. Sprinkle crumb mixture over chiles and cheese. Cover with waxed paper; microwave on 100% (high) 4 minutes, rotate dish after 2 minutes. Sprinkle with remaining cheese. Cover; microwave on 100% (high) 30 seconds or until cheese melts. To test for doneness, insert a wooden pick into center. If it comes out clean, it is done. If more cooking is needed, cover; microwave on 100% (high) 1 minute. Let stand 5 minutes.

Each serving contains:

Cal	Prot	Carb	Fib	Tot. Fat	Sat. Fat	Chol	Sodium
198	12g	10g	0	12g	6g	130mg	281mg

Guacamole

Avocado Dip

Guacamole is used as a garnish for all types of Mexican dishes. Pick a soft avocado or see below for how to soften an avocado.

Servings: 1/2 to 3/4 cup

1 avocado

2 tablespoons chopped onion

1/4 cup Taco Sauce, page 9

Peel and seed avocado; place avocado in a small bowl. Mash avocado with a fork. Add onion and Taco Sauce; stir to combine. Guacamole is ready to serve.

To peel an avocado, cut in 4 lengthwise sections cutting through to the pit. Starting at the narrow end peel each quarter of the avocado by pulling off the skin. The flesh should loosen from the pit. If not, use a knife to pry it from the pit.

Cut the avocado into 1/2-inch cubes or mash it. Prepare the avocado just before serving so it will not discolor. Lemon or lime juice squeezed over the avocado helps preserve its color.

Each tablespoon contains:

Cal	Prot	Carb	Fib	Tot. Fat	Sat. Fat	Chol	Sodium
30	0	2g	2g	3g	0	0	10mg

If avocados are just a little under-ripe, put them in the microwave on 50% (medium) 30 to 45 seconds, rotating after 15 to 20 seconds. Repeat process if needed.

Drying Green Chiles

A wonderful way to prepare fresh chiles from your garden.

Power level: medium-high
Cooking time: 12 to 14 minutes
Servings: 3/4 cup

5 or 6 whole roasted chiles, page 3, or 6 canned whole green chiles

Cut a lengthwise slit along each chile; remove stems, seeds and membranes. Place chiles on paper towels to drain.

Line bottom of a 12" x 8" casserole with paper towels. Open slit chiles and place in lined dish; microwave on 70% (medium-high) 6 to 7 minutes. Remove chiles by lifting paper towels; set chiles aside. Place fresh paper towels in casserole. Return chiles to lined casserole. Microwave on 70% (medium-high) another 6 to 7 minutes. Dried chiles should have a paper-like texture. If chiles are not completely dried, repeat procedure.

Each tablespoon contains:

Cal	Prot	Carb	Fib	Tot. Fat	Sat. Fat	Chol	Sodium
8	0	2g	0	0	0	0	1mg

The traditional way of drying roasted green chiles was to clean pods of stems and seeds; then thread pods on a string and hang them outside in a well-ventilated area. After chiles have been dried, they can be used as a condiment or for Chile Pasado, page 24. They can also be frozen for later use.

Chile Pasado

Dried Green Chile

Serve this tasty condiment with your favorite meat dishes.

Power level: high, medium-high
Cooking time: 4 minutes
Servings: 1 cup

3/4 cup dried green chiles, page 23

1 cup water

1 tablespoon vegetable oil

1/4 cup chopped onion

1 garlic clove, chopped

1/8 teaspoon cilantro seeds, crushed

1/4 teaspoon dried-leaf oregano, crushed

1 tomato, blanched, chopped

1/2 teaspoon salt

Break dried chiles into small pieces; place in a small bowl. Soak chiles in warm water 15 minutes or until softened. Drain and discard liquid; set chiles aside.

Combine oil, onion, garlic, cilantro and oregano in a 1-1/2-quart casserole. Cover with waxed paper; microwave on 100% (high) 2 minutes. Add soaked chiles, tomato and salt to onion mixture. Cover with waxed paper; microwave on 70% (medium-high) 2 minutes. Stir mixture well. Serve hot or cold.

Each tablespoon contains:

Cal	Prot	Carb	Fib	Tot. Fat	Sat. Fat	Chol	Sodium
16	0	2g	0	1g	0	0	68mg

❦ **Variation**
Chile Pasado con Queso
Dried Green Chile with Cheese

Stir 1/2 cup shredded Monterey Jack cheese into 1 cup Chile Pasado. Microwave on 100% (high) 45 seconds. Stir well and serve.

Chile Pasado

Chile pasado is dehydrated chile. The chile is dried after the growing season and used during winter months. Other dried vegetables and fruits are collectively called *orejones*, meaning "long ears" because of their similarity to ears. One popular dish made with dried chiles and dried squash is called *Orejones de Calabaza*. The dehydrated squash and dried chiles are combined with corn to make a dish similar to succotash. The squash is first soaked and drained, then added to the prepared chile pasado with either canned or frozen corn. Although green chiles dry well in a microwave oven, page 23, I have been unsuccessful in drying squash in a microwave. Dry squash by hanging it outside "clothes-line style" or use a food dehydrator.

Caldo de Chile Colorado Fresco

Fresh Red Chile Soup

I recommend using fresh red chiles. If they are not available, use dried red chiles.

Power level: high
Cooking time: 17 minutes
Servings: 4

6 fresh red chiles or 12 dried red chiles

3 cups water

1/2 teaspoon salt

1 tablespoon all-purpose flour

2 tablespoons margarine

1/4 cup chopped onion

1 garlic clove, chopped

1/4 teaspoon cumin

1-1/2 cups shredded Monterey Jack cheese (6 oz.)

Roast and peel fresh chiles, page 3. Remove chile stems and seeds. In a blender, combine chiles, water, salt and flour. Process until smooth; set mixture aside.

Combine margarine, onion, garlic and cumin in a small glass dish. Cover with waxed paper; microwave on 100% (high) 2 minutes. Combine red-chile mixture and onion mixture in a 2-1/2-quart casserole. Cover with waxed paper; microwave on 100% (high) 15 minutes, stirring after 7-1/2 minutes. Stir in cheese at once. Serve hot.

Each serving contains:

Cal	Prot	Carb	Fib	Tot. Fat	Sat. Fat	Chol	Sodium
236	12g	9g	1g	17g	9g	37g	569mg

Comidas de Masa

Mexican cooking practices were largely adapted from native Indian techniques, such as the old method of grinding corn. Women ground corn on a *metate* or volcanic concave stone, using a *mano,* a cylindrical hand-held stone.

The smell of freshly baked flour tortillas is hard to hide, especially from children. As a child, I was always present when tortillas were being baked. Watching the process was half the fun. Whoever was making the tortillas would rhythmically slap a ball of dough from hand to hand, forming a big round tortilla. The tortilla was baked on the *comal* or hot griddle. We knew that eventually we would be handed a hot, buttered tortilla. The only problem was—one tortilla wasn't enough. If we were told that we were only getting one, the game of snitching extras would begin.

Included in these recipes is a master mix for tortillas. You will find them a staple for many of the recipes.

Traditional etiquette among Mexican people is to use the tortilla as a spoon. My father developed a special method of making spoons from the tortilla to use in eating Caldillo and Carne con Chile Colorado. He would tear a piece from a flour tortilla and form a *cucharita,* Spanish for small spoon. He would roll the piece of tortilla into a cone and fold it shut at one end. The open end formed the spoon.

Tamales Dulces

Sweet Tamales

These are served as dessert at festive occasions. I enjoy them for breakfast with Café Mexicana.

Power level: high
Cooking time: 4 minutes for filling
　　　 10 minutes per dozen
Servings: 12 tamales

1/4 lb. corn husks

1 (20-oz.) can unsweetened crushed pineapple

1 cup masa harina

1/3 cup yellow or white cornmeal

3 tablespoons vegetable oil

3 tablespoons sugar

1/4 teaspoon ground cinnamon

1/4 teaspoon anise seeds, crushed

1/4 teaspoon salt

2 tablespoons brown sugar

1/4 cup raisins

1/4 cup water

1/4 teaspoon ground cinnamon

2 tablespoons cornstarch

3 tablespoons pecan pieces

Soak corn husks in water at least 2 hours or until pliable. For dough, drain pineapple juice into a 2-cup measure. Add enough water to make 1 cup liquid. Combine masa harina, cornmeal, vegetable oil, 3 tablespoons sugar, 1/4 teaspoon cinnamon, anise seeds, salt and pineapple liquid in a large mixer bowl. Beat until a soft dough is formed; set dough aside.

To prepare filling, combine drained crushed pineapple, 2 tablespoons brown sugar, raisins, water, 1/4 teaspoon cinnamon, cornstarch and nuts, in a glass bowl. Cover with waxed paper; microwave on 100% (high) 4 minutes, stirring mixture after 2 minutes. Set aside.

Fill and cook tamales using conventional microwave method or microwave pressure cooker, pages 30-31. Serve after cooking or store in freezer up to 3 months. Thaw and reheat to serve.

Each tamale contains:

Cal	Prot	Carb	Fib	Tot. Fat	Sat. Fat	Chol	Sodium
76	1g	13g	1g	3g	0	0	24mg

Tamales

Tamales originated from corn dishes dating back to the Aztec Empire. Making tamales was a community project in our neighborhood. I remember watching women preparing tamales for the church bazaar. They stationed themselves around the kitchen to make an assembly line, each doing a particular task. Several steps were required in making tamales: softening corn husks, dough preparation, adding filling and cooking. The conventional cooking method took about 1 hour, but cooking tamales today in a microwave takes only 10 minutes!

I was too young to keep count, but I recall seeing many paper bags, each filled with a dozen tamales to be sold at the church bazaar. Tamales made for the bazaar were always red-chile tamales because they were everyone's favorite. Contrary to convention, I particularly liked the *Tamales Dulces* or Sweet Tamales.

Two basic tamale recipes are given in this book. However, there is a wide variety of tamale recipes in Mexican cuisine which can be made in the microwave using the same methods provided in these recipes.

The type of tamale determines the selection of the dough and filling. Red-Chile Tamales are made with red-chile filling and red-chile-based dough. Green-Chile Tamales are made with green-chile filling and green-chile-based dough. Sweet tamales are made with sweet filling and sweet dough. Use the appropriate dough and filling when making your favorite tamales.

Tamales

For more flavor add shredded cheese and olives.

Power level: high
Cooking time: 10 minutes
Servings: 12 tamales

1/4 lb. dry corn husks

1 cup masa harina

1/3 cup yellow or white cornmeal

1/4 teaspoon salt

3 tablespoons vegetable oil

1/3 cup Chile Colorado, page 10 or Salsa para Enchiladas Verdes, page 13

1/3 cup beef or chicken broth

1/3 cup water

1 cup shredded, cooked beef, pork or chicken

3/4 cup Chile Colorado, page 10, or Salsa para Enchiladas Verdes, page 13

Tamales can be made with a masa harina dough. Masa harina is a ground corn mixture available at most supermarkets.

Soak corn husks in water at least 2 hours or until pliable. Combine masa harina, cornmeal and salt in a mixing bowl and mix well. Combine oil, 1/3 cup Chile Colorado or Salsa para Enchiladas Verdes, broth and water in a glass measuring cup. Gradually add liquid to dry ingredients while mixing gently until mixture is light and fluffy. Set aside. Combine 1 cup cooked meat with 3/4 cup Chile Colorado or Salsa para Enchiladas Verdes.

Tamales can be cooked by standard microwave method or by using a microwave pressure cooker.

For conventional microwave method, open corn husks; if one husk is not large enough for a tamale, take 2 and overlap them. Spread with 2 tablespoons tamale dough at center of husk. Top with 1 tablespoon tamale filling. Make tamales no more than 4-inches long. They stand in cooking container.

Fold and wrap each tamale as follows: fold bottom of husk over dough and filling, fold sides together, take a thin lengthwise piece of husk and tie top of tamale. Make sure tamale is tied tightly and dough is not exposed, otherwise dough will dry out.

Stand 12 tamales in a 2-quart glass measuring cup; cover with plastic wrap. Pierce plastic wrap so steam will vent during cooking. Microwave on 100% (high) 10 minutes, rotating dish after 5 minutes. Let stand 5 minutes before serving. Tamales can be stored in a freezer up to 3 months. Thaw and reheat for serving.

For a microwave pressure cooker, fill tamales as above. Stand tamales on end in a microwave pressure cooker. To keep tamales from drying out, cut a piece of foil the size of the diameter of the pressure cooker; place over tamales.

Close pressure cooker; put on pressure regulator weight. Microwave on 100% (high) 10 minutes. Let pressure cooker stand with pressure 5 minutes. If pressure cooker has a pressure-indicating gauge or stem, standing time should be the time it takes for indicator to show pressure has dropped. Remove pressure-regulator weight; open pressure cooker. Tamales are ready to serve. Tamales can be stored in a freezer up to 3 months. Thaw and reheat for serving.

Each tamale contains:

Cal	Prot	Carb	Fib	Tot. Fat	Sat. Fat	Chol	Sodium
132	6g	15g	2g	6g	1g	11mg	95mg

Caution: Some microwave ovens may not tolerate any metal during operation. Check your microwave oven owner's manual before using foil.
Broth: If using the broth from cooked meat, freeze the broth in a shallow dish. This allows removal of fat from the surface.
Corn husks: Any used corn husks can be washed, laid out flat and sun-dried to be used again for tamales. Re-soak the husks to soften them.
Frozen Tamales: Tamales can be made and frozen up to 3 months. Tamales can be frozen uncooked. To cook, remove frozen tamales and allow to thaw. Place tamales in an upright position in a deep bowl or measuring cup, cover with plastic wrap, folding one edge of the wrap over for ventilation, and microwave on 100% (high) for one minute for each tamale being cooked.

Photo back cover

Enchiladas

Quick way to prepare those always-favorite enchiladas.

Power level: high, medium-high
Cooking time: 14 to 18 minutes
Servings: 6

3 cups cooked Chile Colorado, page 10

1 lb. ground beef or ground turkey

3/4 teaspoon ground cumin

1-1/2 teaspoons onion powder

1/4 teaspoon ground oregano

1 teaspoon garlic powder

1/2 teaspoon salt

12 (6-inch) corn tortillas

2 tablespoons vegetable oil

1-1/2 cups shredded Cheddar cheese (6 oz.)

1/2 cup chopped onion

2 cups shredded lettuce

1/2 cup chopped tomatoes

Place Chile Colorado in a flat-bottom casserole; microwave on 100% (high) 2 minutes; set aside. Crumble ground beef or turkey into a 1-1/2-quart casserole or microwave browning dish. Cover with waxed paper; microwave on 100% (high) 5 to 6 minutes, stirring after 3 minutes. Meat is done when no longer pink. Drain fat; add cumin, onion powder, oregano, garlic powder and salt; mix well; set meat mixture aside.

Rub both sides of each tortilla with oil; place in 2 stacks of 6 tortillas each. Wrap each stack in waxed paper; microwave 1 stack on 100% (high) 50 seconds. Remove tortillas; repeat for remaining stack.

Grease or spray with vegetable cooking spray a 12" x 8" flat casserole. Dip each softened tortilla into chile sauce. Spoon 2 heaping tablespoons meat in center of tortilla; sprinkle a little cheese and onion.

Roll tortilla tightly; place seam-side down in casserole. Repeat for all tortillas. Pour remaining sauce over filled and rolled tortillas. Sprinkle with remaining onion and cheese.

Cover with waxed paper; microwave on 70% (medium-high) 5 to
8 minutes or until enchiladas are hot
and bubbly, rotating dish after 3 minutes. Let stand 1 minute. Garnish
with lettuce and tomatoes.

Each serving contains:

Cal	Prot	Carb	Fib	Tot. Fat	Sat. Fat	Chol	Sodium
558	33g	43g	8g	31g	12g	96mg	578mg

❦ Variation
Vegetarian Enchiladas

Omit beef. Substitute 1 1/2 cups cottage or ricotta cheese. Add 1 (10 oz.)
pkg. frozen chopped spinach or
broccoli, cooked, well drained.
Follow directions above. Garnish
with sliced radish.

❦ ❦ ❦

*My mother served red-chile enchila-
das at least once a week. They were
also popular as a pre-game meal for
the football crowd. She would top
the stack of enchiladas with a fried
egg. This is the traditional way of
serving enchiladas in Southern New
Mexico. There is a degree of region-
alism in Mexican cuisine between
Texas-Coahuila or Tex-Mex, New
Mexico-Chihuahua, Arizona-
Sonora, and California-Baja. But in
all cases, chile remains the
dominant ingredient.*

Enchiladas Verdes

Green Enchiladas

*For Sour-cream Enchiladas, stir 1
cup sour cream into heated salsa.*

Power level: medium-high, high
Cooking time: 10 to 13 minutes
Servings: 4

**2 cups Salsa para Enchiladas
Verdes, page 13**

12 (6-inch) corn tortillas

1 tablespoon vegetable oil

**1-1/2 cups shredded Cheddar
cheese (6 oz.)**

1/2 cup chopped onion

1 cup shredded lettuce

1/2 cup chopped tomatoes

❦ **Variations**
Enchiladas de Pollo

Chicken Enchiladas

Stir 2 cups shredded cooked
chicken, 1/2 cup chicken broth and
1/2 cup evaporated skimmed milk
into enchilada sauce. Continue as
directed above.

Pour enchilada salsa in a flat
casserole. Cover with waxed paper;
microwave on 70% (medium-high)
3 minutes. Set sauce aside.

Rub both sides of tortillas with oil or
water. Wrap 6 tortillas in waxed
paper; microwave on 100% (high)
50 seconds. Remove tortillas; repeat
for remaining tortillas.

Grease or spray with vegetable cooking spray a 12" x 8" flat casserole.
Dip each tortilla in salsa. Place tortilla in casserole; sprinkle with cheese
and onion. Top with another tortilla.
Repeat; making 2 stacks of 6 tortillas
each. Top with remaining sauce.

Cover with waxed paper; microwave on 70% (medium-high) 5 to
8 minutes or until cheese melts,
rotating dish after 3 minutes. Garnish with lettuce and tomatoes.
Serve immediately.

Each serving contains:

Cal	Prot	Carb	Fib	Tot. Fat	Sat. Fat	Chol	Sodium
470	18g	49g	9g	24g	10g	45mg	272mg

Tortillas de Harina

Flour Tortillas

Fresh flour tortillas make any meal special.

Power level: high
Cooking time: 6-1/2 minutes
Servings: 1 dozen

4 cups all-purpose flour

2 teaspoons baking power

2 teaspoons salt

4 tablespoons vegetable oil

1-1/2 cups warm water

❦ **Variation**
For wheat tortillas, substitute 2 cups whole-wheat flour for 2 cups all-purpose flour. Follow recipe as given.

Flour tortillas can also be cooked on a griddle or an electric skillet.

Combine flour, baking powder and salt in a bowl. Add oil; blend until mixture is crumbly. Gradually add water, blend forming a ball. If dough is dry, add 1 tablespoon water, then work dough. Repeat if necessary. Turn dough out onto a lightly floured board; knead 5 minutes. Cover; let stand 30 minutes. Divide dough into 12 balls. On a lightly floured board, roll each ball into an 8-inch circle. Stack tortillas, separating each with waxed paper.

Heat a microwave browning dish on 100% (high) 5 minutes. Place a tortilla on the hot browning dish; microwave on 100% (high) 35 seconds. Turn tortilla over; microwave on 100% (high) another 35 seconds. Remove tortilla; place on a damp cloth. Fold cloth to cover tortilla. Repeat for remaining tortillas. If necessary, reheat the browning dish every third or fourth tortilla. Tortillas are ready to use or store in a reclosable plastic bag in the refrigerator 4 to 7 days.

Each tortilla contains:

Cal	Prot	Carb	Fib	Tot. Fat	Sat. Fat	Chol	Sodium
193	4g	32g	1g	5g	0	0	411mg

Burritos

Burros, *as they are sometimes called, are made by filling a large flour tortilla with a bean and/or meat mixture.*

Power level: high
Cooking time: 13 to 16 minutes
Servings: 6

1 lb. ground beef

2 tablespoons vegetable oil

2 tablespoons red-chile powder

1/4 cup chopped onion

1 garlic clove, chopped

1/2 teaspoon salt

1/4 teaspoon dried-leaf oregano, crushed

12 (10-inch) flour tortillas

2 cups Frijoles Puré, page 63, or 1 (16 oz.) can refried beans

1-1/2 cups shredded Cheddar cheese (6 oz.)

Crumble ground beef into a 2-quart casserole. Cover with waxed paper; microwave on 100% (high) 4 to 5 minutes, stirring after 2 minutes. Meat is done when it is no longer pink. Drain off fat; set meat aside.

Combine oil, chile powder, onion, garlic, salt and oregano in a 1-1/2-quart casserole. Cover; microwave on 100% (high) 2 minutes. Add beef, blending well. Cover; microwave on 100% (high) 3 to 4 minutes.

To soften tortillas, moisten both sides of each tortilla with water; place in 2 stacks of 6 tortillas each. Wrap each stack in waxed paper; microwave 1 stack on 100% (high) 50 seconds. Remove tortillas; repeat for remaining stack.

Grease or spray with vegetable cooking spray a 12" x 8" flat-bottom casserole. Spread 2 tablespoons beans on a tortilla. Top with 2 tablespoons meat. Sprinkle with a little cheese. Roll tortilla tightly; place seam-side down in casserole. Repeat for all tortillas. Cover; microwave on 100% (high) 2 to 3 minutes. Serve.

Each serving contains:

Cal	Prot	Carb	Fib	Tot. Fat	Sat. Fat	Chol	Sodium
850	44g	84g	11g	41g	15g	105mg	930mg

Tacos de Carne

Beef Tacos

Tacos are fried corn tortillas folded in half, filled with meat and topped with cheese and condiments.

Power level: high, medium-high
Cooking time: 10 to 11 minutes
Servings: 6

1-1/2 lbs. ground beef or ground turkey

1/4 cup chopped onion

3 tablespoons Taco Seasoning Mix, page 8, or 1 (1-1/4-oz.) pkg. taco seasoning mix

1 (8-oz.) can tomato sauce

12 Taco Shells, page 43, or commercial shells

1-1/2 cups shredded Cheddar cheese (6 oz.)

2 cups shredded lettuce

1 cup chopped tomatoes

1 cup Taco Sauce, page 9

Crumble ground beef or ground turkey into a 2-quart casserole. Blend in onion. Cover with waxed paper; microwave on 100% (high) 4 minutes, stirring after 2 minutes. Meat is cooked when it is no longer pink. Drain off fat. Stir in taco seasoning mix and tomato sauce. Cover with waxed paper; microwave on 70% (medium-high) 5 to 6 minutes, stirring after 3 minutes. Spoon meat mixture into each taco shell. Place filled shells upright in a flat-bottom casserole. Top with cheese. Microwave on 100% (high) 1 minute or until cheese melts. Garnish with lettuce and tomatoes. Serve with Taco Sauce.

Each serving contains:

Cal	Prot	Carb	Fib	Tot. Fat	Sat. Fat	Chol	Sodium
605	41g	38g	8g	34g	15g	128mg	532mg

Tacos de Pollo

Chicken Tacos

A great way to use cooked chicken and a welcome change from the traditional beef taco.

Power level: high
Cooking time: 3 minutes
Servings: 6

3/4 cup chopped onion

2 tablespoons vegetable oil

3 cups shredded cooked chicken

**12 Taco Shells, page 43, or
   commercial shells**

**1-1/2 cups shredded Cheddar
   cheese (6 oz.)**

2 cups shredded lettuce

1 cup chopped tomatoes

1 cup Taco Sauce, page 9

Combine 1/4 cup onion and oil in a 1-1/2-quart casserole. Cover with waxed paper; microwave on 100% (high) 2 minutes. Stir in cooked chicken; spoon mixture into taco shells; place filled shells upright in a flat-bottom casserole. Top with cheese. Microwave on 100% (high) 1 minute or until cheese melts. Sprinkle with lettuce, tomatoes and remaining 1/2 cup onion. Serve with Taco Sauce.

Each serving contains:

Cal	Prot	Carb	Fib	Tot. Fat	Sat. Fat	Chol	Sodium
443	32g	34g	7g	21g	8g	88mg	294mg

Tostadas

Tostadas are flat, crisp corn tortillas topped with a tasty bean mixture.

Power level: high
Cooking time: 2 minutes each
Servings: 4

8 (6-inch) corn tortillas

2 tablespoons vegetable oil or water

1 cup Frijoles Puré, page 63, or 1/2 (16-oz.) can refried beans, heated

1-1/2 cups shredded Cheddar cheese (6 oz.)

2 cups shredded lettuce

1 cup coarsely chopped tomatoes

1/2 cup chopped onion

1 cup Taco Sauce, page 9

Rub both sides of each tortilla lightly with oil or water; place on waxed paper. Microwave each tortilla on 100% (high) 1-1/2 minutes or until crisp. Spread 1 to 2 tablespoons beans on a tortilla. Cover with waxed paper; microwave on 100% (high) 30 seconds. Top with cheese, lettuce, tomatoes, onion and Taco Sauce. Repeat for each remaining tortilla. Serve immediately.

Each serving contains:

Cal	Prot	Carb	Fib	Tot. Fat	Sat. Fat	Chol	Sodium
517	24g	52g	13g	26g	11g	52mg	415mg

Quesadillas

Cheese-Filled Tortillas

Here's a quick and easy snack.
Great for children to prepare.

Power level: high
Cooking time: 1-1/2 minutes each
Servings: 6

12 (6-inch) corn or (8-inch)
flour tortillas

2 tablespoons vegetable oil

2 cups shredded Monterey Jack
or Cheddar cheese (8 oz.)

Rub both sides of each tortilla lightly with oil; place on waxed paper or a paper plate. Microwave each tortilla on 100% (high) 45 seconds. Sprinkle cheese on hot tortilla; fold tortilla in half. Microwave on 100% (high) 35 seconds or until cheese melts. Repeat procedure for each tortilla. Serve immediately.

Each serving contains:

Cal	Prot	Carb	Fib	Tot. Fat	Sat. Fat	Chol	Sodium
311	13g	26g	5g	18g	8g	33mg	204mg

Quesadillas are my favorite cheese-filled tortilla. Traditionally, Quesadillas are made with goat cheese called asadero. *I substitute Monterey Jack or mild Cheddar cheese for the asadero. My children quickly learned to prepare Quesadillas in the microwave.*

Chile con Queso Nachos

Cheese Dip Nachos

Having a party? Here's a superb party snack.

Power level: medium-high
Cooking time: 30 seconds per serving
Servings: 4 to 6

16 (6-inch) corn tortillas, prepared as chips, page 44, or 1 (11-oz.) pkg. tortilla chips

2 cups Frijoles Puré, page 63, or 1 (16-oz.) can refried beans

2 cups shredded Cheddar cheese (8 oz.)

1 cup Taco Sauce, page 9, or PACE® Picante Sauce

Prepare microwave tortilla chips. Spread beans on each tortilla chip. Top with cheese. Place 12 chips on a paper plate; microwave on 70% (medium-high) 30 seconds or until cheese melts. Repeat for remaining chips. Pour Taco Sauce or Picante Sauce over chips. Serve immediately.

Each serving contains:

Cal	Prot	Carb	Fib	Tot. Fat	Sat. Fat	Chol	Sodium
487	25g	59g	14g	19g	10g	50mg	363mg

Compuestas

Cheese Crisps Deluxe

Cheese crisps, also known as tostadas, *can be dressed up with a variety of toppings.*

Power level: high
Cooking time: 1-1/2 minutes each
Servings: 2 to 4

4 (8-inch) flour tortillas

2 tablespoons margarine

1 cup Frijoles Puré, page 63, or 1/2 (16-oz.) can refried beans

1 cup shredded Cheddar cheese (4 oz.)

1 cup Taco Sauce, page 9

1/2 cup shredded lettuce

1/2 cup chopped tomatoes

1/4 cup sliced ripe olives

1/4 cup chopped onion

Spread both sides of each tortilla lightly with margarine. Place 1 tortilla on waxed paper or a paper plate; microwave on 100% (high) 40 seconds. Spread hot tortilla with 1/4 cup beans; sprinkle with 1/4 cup cheese. Microwave on 100% (high) 30 to 40 seconds or until cheese melts. Top with 1/4 cup Taco Sauce, 2 tablespoons each of lettuce and tomatoes, and 1 tablespoon each of olives and onion. Repeat for each remaining tortilla. Serve hot.

Each serving contains:

Cal	Prot	Carb	Fib	Tot. Fat	Sat. Fat	Chol	Sodium
402	19g	42g	8g	20g	9g	37mg	527mg

Taco Shells

The trick is to microwave the tortilla in the shape of a shell.

Power level: high
Cooking time: 3 to 4 minutes
Servings: 5 taco shells

5 (6-inch) corn tortillas

Vegetable oil

Method 1
Rub both sides of each tortilla lightly with oil; stack tortillas. Wrap stack with waxed paper; microwave on 100% (high) 50 seconds. While soft, fold each tortilla over the rim of a large bowl. Microwave on 100% (high) 3 to 4 minutes, turning bowl each minute. Desired softness or crispness of the tortilla will determine length of cooking time. Remove tortillas from bowl; they should be the half-circle shape of a taco shell.

Fill taco shells with your favorite fillings; top with lettuce, cheese, chopped tomatoes and salsa.

Method 2
Taco shells are also formed by using a microwave-safe ceramic taco server. These are available at kitchenware and department stores.

Fill server with softened tortillas with edges facing up. If they are too limp, support them with wooden picks. Follow directions above.

Each shell contains:

Cal	Prot	Carb	Fib	Tot. Fat	Sat. Fat	Chol	Sodium
65	2g	13g	2g	1g	0	0	1mg

Tortilla Chips

Homemade are the best!

Power level: high
Cooking time: 6 minutes
Servings: 36 chips

6 (6-inch) corn tortillas

4 teaspoons vegetable oil

Salt to taste

Cut each tortilla into 6 pie-shape wedges. Place half the tortilla wedges in a single layer in a 12" x 8" flat-bottom casserole. Coat wedges with oil; microwave on 100% (high) 3 minutes. Drain wedges on paper towels; salt to taste. Repeat for remaining tortilla wedges. Serve warm.

Each chip contains:

Cal	Prot	Carb	Fib	Tot. Fat	Sat. Fat	Chol	Sodium
15	0g	2g	0g	1g	0	0	0

❦ Variation
Seasoned Tortilla Chips

Prepare chips as above. Place chips in a large plastic bag; add 3 table-spoons Taco Seasoning Mix, page 8, or 1 (1-1/4-oz.) pkg. taco seasoning mix. Shake bag lightly until chips are well coated. Shake off excess seasoning. Serve immediately.

If counting calories: instead of coating tortilla wedges with oil, moisten each one with water.

Crispas

Crispies

A sweet, cinnamon-flavored crisp tortilla that's a real favorite when served at parties.

Power level: high
Cooking time: 2 minutes per plate
Servings: 6

6 (8-inch) flour tortillas

2 tablespoons vegetable oil

1/2 cup sugar

1 teaspoon ground cinnamon

Rub both sides of each tortilla lightly with oil. Cut each tortilla in 6 pie-shape wedges.

Grease or spray with vegetable cooking spray a 12" x 8" flat-bottom casserole. Place 8 or 9 tortilla wedges in casserole; microwave on 100% (high) 1 minute. Turn wedges over; microwave on 100% (high) 1 minute or until crisp.

Combine sugar and cinnamon in a small bowl; dip each hot tortilla wedge in sugar mixture. Repeat for remaining tortilla wedges.

To prepare crispies using a microwave browning dish. Heat browning dish on 100% (high) 4 minutes. Place 8 tortilla wedges in hot browning dish; microwave on 100% (high) 1 minute. Turn wedges over; microwave on 100% (high) 1 minute. When crisp, dip in sugar and cinnamon mixture.

Each serving contains:

Cal	Prot	Carb	Fib	Tot. Fat	Sat. Fat	Chol	Sodium
210	3g	36g	1g	7g	1g	0	135mg

Chimichangas

Crisp Burritos

Chimichangas are a popular deep-fried burrito.

Power level: high
Cooking time: 5 minutes
Servings: 5

5 (8-inch) flour tortillas

Vegetable oil or water

3/4 cup Machaca, page 80; Frijoles Puré, page 63; or ground beef

1/3 cup Chile Colorado, page 10, or Salsa Para Enchiladas Verdes, page 13

1/2 cup shredded Cheddar cheese (2 oz.)

Condiments of your choice

Rub both sides of each tortilla with oil or water; stack tortillas. Wrap stack with waxed paper; microwave on 100% (high) 50 seconds. Spread 2 tablespoons filling in center of each tortilla; top with 1 tablespoon sauce. Sprinkle with cheese.

Fold bottom edge of tortilla up; fold sides over filling; then fold top of tortilla down. Brush outer surface of chimichanga with vegetable oil. Repeat for remaining chimichangas.

Heat a microwave browning dish on 100% (high) 4 minutes. Place 5 chimichangas in hot browning dish; microwave on 100% (high) 4 minutes or until crisp, turning after 2 minutes and rotating dish. Serve with your favorite condiments.

Each serving contains:

Cal	Prot	Carb	Fib	Tot. Fat	Sat. Fat	Chol	Sodium
196	11g	22g	1g	8g	3g	28mg	265mg

❦   ❦   ❦

When I moved to Arizona I learned about Chimichangas. Since my first taste, I have been addicted. My recipe is a rendition of the Arizona Chimichanga.

Caldo de Tortillas

Tortilla Soup

A great soup to begin any meal.

Power level: high
Cooking time: 12 minutes
Servings: 4 cups

1 tablespoon vegetable oil

1/4 cup chopped onion

1 garlic clove, chopped

1/4 teaspoon cumin

4 cups chicken broth or 4 chicken bouillon cubes dissolved in 4 cups hot water

5 (6-inch) corn tortillas, cut in 1-inch pieces

1/4 cup chopped green chiles

Salt to taste

2 tablespoons chopped fresh cilantro or parsley

Combine oil, onion, garlic and cumin in a 2-quart glass bowl. Cover with waxed paper; microwave on 100% (high) 2 minutes. Add broth, tortillas and chiles to onion mixture. Cover with waxed paper; microwave on 100% (high) 10 minutes, stirring after 5 minutes. Season to taste. Garnish with cilantro or parsley. Serve hot.

Each serving contains:

Cal	Prot	Carb	Fib	Tot. Fat	Sat. Fat	Chol	Sodium
159	8g	19g	3g	6g	1g	1mg	2mg

Chalupas

Little Canoes

Microwave a corn tortilla to form a canoe or "shallow boat." Fill with tasty meat, beans and add toppings.

Power level: high
Cooking time: 18 to 19 minutes
Servings: 8 chalupas

8 corn tortillas

1 lb. ground turkey or ground beef

3 tablespoons Taco Seasoning Mix, page 8, or 1 (1-1/4-oz.) pkg. taco seasoning mix

1 cup Frijoles Puré, page 63, or 1 (16-oz.) can refried beans

1/2 cup chopped onion

1 cup chopped tomatoes

1 cup shredded lettuce

1 cup Taco Sauce, page 9, or Chile Colorado, page 10

1/2 cup shredded Cheddar cheese (2 oz.)

To heat tortillas, see Enchiladas Verdes, page 34, paragraph 2.

Lightly coat a 6- to 7-inch diameter microwave-safe soup bowl with vegetable coating spray. Place softened tortilla in bowl bottom and microwave on 100% (high) 1-1/2 to 2 minutes until crisp. Repeat for remaining tortillas. Set aside.

Put turkey or beef in a 2-quart casserole dish and stir in seasoning mix. Cover with waxed paper, microwave on 100% (high) 5 minutes, stir after 2-1/2 minutes. Drain. Add beans, microwave on 100% (high) 1-1/2 minutes.

Fill each chalupa with turkey and beans. Top with onions, tomatoes, lettuce, Taco Sauce or Chile Colorado and cheese.

Each serving contains:

Cal	Prot	Carb	Fib	Tot. Fat	Sat. Fat	Chol	Sodium
278	19g	28g	7g	11g	4g	41mg	298mg

Pan de Maíz

Mexican Corn Bread

Corn bread is a tasty treat with beans and makes a real hearty meal.

Power level: medium, high
Cooking time: 10 to 11 minutes
Servings: 8

1 cup cornmeal

1/2 cup all-purpose flour

1 tablespoon baking powder

1 teaspoon salt

1 (8-1/2-oz.) can cream-style corn

1/4 cup vegetable oil

2 eggs

1/4 cup chopped green chiles or 1 (4-oz.) can diced green chiles

1 cup shredded mild Cheddar cheese (4 oz.)

Combine cornmeal, flour, baking powder and salt in a bowl. Stir in corn, oil, eggs, chiles and cheese. Grease a microwave-safe ring mold or a round, glass cake dish. Place an inverted custard cup in center of cake dish. Pour batter into greased mold or cake dish.

Microwave on 50% (medium) 5 minutes, turning after 2-1/2 minutes. Microwave on 100% (high) an additional 5 to 6 minutes, turning dish after 2-1/2 minutes. Let stand 5 minutes. Corn bread is done when a wooden pick inserted in center comes out clean. Serve warm with butter.

Each serving contains:

Cal	Prot	Carb	Fib	Tot. Fat	Sat. Fat	Chol	Sodium
253	8g	26g	2g	13g	4g	68mg	580mg

Panecillos de Maíz Azul

Blue-corn Muffins with Chile

Great topped with either pinto or black beans. Yellow cornmeal can be substituted for blue cornmeal.

Power level: medium
Cooking time: 5 minutes
Servings: 12

1-1/2 cups blue cornmeal

1 tablespoon baking powder

1/2 teaspoon salt

3 tablespoons vegetable oil

1/4 cup chopped green chiles or 1 (4-oz.) can diced green chiles

2 tablespoons chopped onion or 1/4 teaspoon onion powder

2 eggs or 3 egg whites

3/4 cup skim milk

Blue corn is a traditional Southwestern ingredient with authentic flavor. The current popularity of blue corn is due to its rich toasted, nutty flavor and unusual color. As a bonus, it is also high in protein.

In a bowl combine all ingredients. Grease with cooking oil or spray with vegetable cooking spray a 6-cup microwave-safe cupcake dish or use paper baking cups. Fill each cup 2/3 full.

Microwave on 50% (medium) 5 minutes, turning dish after 2-1/2 minutes. Let stand 5 minutes. Muffins are done when a toothpick inserted in center comes out clean. If muffins are not done, microwave on 50% (medium) another 1 to 2 minutes until done. Repeat for remaining muffin batter.

Each serving contains:

Cal	Prot	Carb	Fib	Tot. Fat	Sat. Fat	Chol	Sodium
114	3g	15g	1g	5g	1g	36mg	190mg

❧ Variation
To make into bread follow instructions for Pan de Maíz on page 49.

Comidas de Huevos

Desayuno, or breakfast, as known in the Southwest, was a very important meal in my family. I remember my dad having eggs with chorizo or scrambled eggs with green chile, served with a hot tortilla.

Chorizo sausage originated in Spain. The chorizo my mother bought was pork sausage heavily seasoned with red chile and other Mexican seasonings. The outer casing was peeled before the filling could be fried.

My favorite egg dish has always been Huevos Rancheros con Chile Colorado. I place a flour tortilla on a plate, top it with cooked eggs and Chile Colorado.

Many spices and ingredients are added to eggs in Mexican dishes. Eggs are a complete meal when eaten with beans, rice, tortillas and your favorite salsa.

Do not attempt to cook an egg in its shell in the microwave oven. Pressure will build up inside the shell, causing the egg to explode. You'll have a terrible mess to clean up in your microwave oven.

The egg yolk cooks faster than the white in a microwave oven. Therefore, the egg yolk should be pricked with a toothpick or fork before microwaving. If the egg yolk is not pricked prior to cooking, the egg yolk may explode, creating a mess in your microwave oven.

Huevos Rancheros con Chile Colorado

Ranch-style Eggs with Red Chile

Simply delicious served over a flour tortilla; my favorite way to have eggs.

Power level: high, medium-high
Cooking time: 4 to 5 minutes
Servings: 2

1 cup Chile Colorado, page 10

1 tablespoon vegetable oil

2 eggs

Combine Chile Colorado and oil in a 9-inch glass pie plate. Cover with waxed paper; microwave on 100% (high) 3 minutes. Carefully break eggs into chile mixture; try to avoid breaking egg yolks.

With a wooden pick, pierce each egg yolk to prevent bursting when cooking. Spoon chile over eggs. Cover with waxed paper; microwave on 70% (medium-high) 45 seconds per egg, rotating dish after 25 seconds.

If eggs are not completely cooked, microwave on 70% (medium-high) another 30 seconds or until eggs are cooked. Season to taste. Serve immediately.

Each serving contains:

Cal	Prot	Carb	Fib	Tot. Fat	Sat. Fat	Chol	Sodium
190	9g	14g	2g	12g	2g	213mg	222mg

Huevos Rancheros con Chile Verde

Ranch-style Eggs with Green Chile

Serve these eggs for breakfast with corn tortillas and refried beans.

Power level: high, medium-high
Cooking time: 4 to 5 minutes
Servings: 2

1 tablespoon vegetable oil

2 tablespoons chopped onion

2 tablespoons chopped bell pepper

1/2 garlic clove, chopped

2 eggs

1/4 cup green-chile strips

1 tablespoon water

1/4 cup shredded Cheddar cheese (1 oz.)

Combine oil, onion, bell pepper and garlic in a 9-inch glass pie plate. Cover with waxed paper; microwave on 100% (high) 2 minutes. Carefully break eggs into onion mixture; try to avoid breaking egg yolks.

With a wooden pick, pierce each egg yolk to prevent bursting when cooking. Top eggs with chile strips; add 1 tablespoon water. Cover with waxed paper; microwave on 70% (medium-high) 2 to 3 minutes or until cooked. Top with cheese. Season to taste. Serve immediately.

Each serving contains:

Cal	Prot	Carb	Fib	Tot. Fat	Sat. Fat	Chol	Sodium
206	10g	4g	1g	17g	5g	228mg	150mg

Torta de Huevo Española

Spanish Omelet

Don't know what to prepare for breakfast? Try this delicious omelet. Cooked bacon or sausage can also be added with the cheese.

Power level: high
Cooking time: 4-1/2 minutes
Servings: 2

2 tablespoons margarine

2 tablespoons chopped onion

2 tablespoons chopped bell pepper

2 tablespoons chopped green chiles

2 eggs or 1 egg plus 2 egg whites

1/4 cup shredded Cheddar cheese (1 oz.)

Combine margarine, onion, bell pepper and chiles in a 9-inch glass pie plate. Cover with waxed paper; microwave on 100% (high) 2 minutes. Spoon into another dish.

Beat eggs together in pie plate; microwave on 100% (high) 1-1/2 minutes, pushing cooked eggs toward center of dish every 30 seconds and allowing uncooked egg to flow to edge of dish.

Add cooked vegetables and cheese; using a spatula, carefully lift egg layer from one side of pie plate and fold in half. Microwave on 100% (high) 1 minute, turning omelet over after 30 seconds. Eggs are done when they are almost set but are still soft. Let stand 1 minute. Season to taste. Serve immediately.

Each serving contains:

Cal	Prot	Carb	Fib	Tot. Fat	Sat. Fat	Chol	Sodium
217	10g	3g	0	18g	7g	228mg	290mg

Huevos con Chorizo

Eggs with Mexican Sausage

A great dish for breakfast; it's delicious served in a warm rolled flour tortilla.

Power level: high
Cooking time: 6 to 8 minutes
Servings: 4

**1/2 lb. Chorizo, page 75, or
   1/2 lb. commercial chorizo**

2 tablespoons chopped onion

4 eggs

Crumble chorizo into a 9-inch glass pie plate; add onion. Cover with waxed paper; microwave on 100% (high) 3 to 4 minutes, stirring after 1-1/2 minutes. Meat should be completely cooked; drain off fat.

Break eggs into cooked chorizo mixture; stir until blended. Cover with waxed paper; microwave on 100% (high) 3 to 4 minutes, stirring mixture from outside to center after 2 minutes. Eggs are done when they are almost set but are still soft. Let stand 1 minute. Season to taste. Serve immediately.

Each serving contains:

Cal	Prot	Carb	Fib	Tot. Fat	Sat. Fat	Chol	Sodium
287	12g	3g	1g	25g	9g	246mg	627mg

Huevos Revueltos con Chile Verde

Scrambled Eggs with Green Chiles

Three simple ingredients turn into a wonderful dish.

Power level: high
Cooking time: 3-1/2 minutes
Servings: 2

2 tablespoons margarine

2 eggs or 1 egg plus 2 egg whites, beaten

1/4 cup chopped green chiles

Place margarine in a 9-inch glass pie plate. Cover with waxed paper; microwave on 100% (high) 1-1/2 minutes or until melted. Stir in eggs and chiles. Cover with waxed paper; microwave on 100% (high) 2 minutes, stirring from outside to center after 1 minute. Eggs are done when they are almost set but are still soft. Let stand 1 minute. Season to taste. Serve immediately.

Each serving contains:

Cal	Prot	Carb	Fib	Tot. Fat	Sat. Fat	Chol	Sodium
159	7g	2g	0	14g	4g	213mg	203mg

Torta de Huevo

Flat Mexican Omelet

My version of the Mexican omelet.

Power level: high
Cooking time: 5 minutes
Servings: 4

1 tablespoon margarine

3 eggs or 1 egg plus 3 egg whites

1/2 cup shredded Cheddar cheese (2 oz.)

2 tablespoons skim milk

2 tablespoons chopped onion

2 tablespoons chopped bell pepper

2 tablespoons chopped green chiles

1/4 cup Taco Sauce, page 9, if desired

Place margarine in a 9-inch glass pie plate; microwave on 100% (high) 40 seconds or until melted. Put eggs, 1/4 cup cheese, milk, onion, bell pepper and chiles in a separate bowl; stir to blend. Pour egg mixture into melted margarine; microwave on 100% (high) 2 minutes.

Push cooked egg mixture toward center of dish every 30 seconds, allowing uncooked egg to flow to edge of dish. Microwave on 100% (high) 2 minutes. Eggs are done when they are almost set but are still soft. Let stand 1 minute. Pour Taco Sauce over eggs, if desired. Top with remaining cheese. Serve immediately.

Each serving contains:

Cal	Prot	Carb	Fib	Tot. Fat	Sat. Fat	Chol	Sodium
146	9g	4g	1g	11g	5g	175mg	197mg

Comidas de Arroz, Frijoles y Pasta

A bowl of beans in its own liquid or Frijoles Puré is usually served with all Mexican meals—breakfast, lunch or supper. They go with any food from meat to chicken, corn dishes, cheese dishes and chile dishes. Two variations, cooked fresh pinto beans and refried beans, are fast and easy to prepare.

The beans I use in my recipes are referred to as *pinto beans*. Before my mother cooked beans, she would have me remove any stones, twigs, dirt or any broken beans. I would then wash the beans and soak them in water for the next day's cooking.

In my family, beans were prepared at the beginning of the week and served as fresh beans in their liquid. After two or three days, my mother would mash the beans and then fry them in a skillet of hot lard or oil, at which time we referred to them as *frijoles refritos* or refried beans.

Beans, a very good source of high-fiber and vegetable protein, are also rich in iron, B-complex vitamins, phosphorous and potassium. Beans do not contain sodium or fat. By adding a grain such as rice or a flour or corn tortilla, beans become a complete protein.

❧   ❧   ❧

In many traditional Mexican recipes, the rice is browned in an ungreased skillet over medium-high heat before adding other ingredients. Or you can add one tablespoon of oil before adding the rice. Stir rice 4 to 5 minutes until the grains are lightly browned.

Rice can be browned in your microwave oven by placing it in a 2-quart casserole dish. Add 1 tablespoon of vegetable oil to the rice and mix to coat it thoroughly. Microwave, uncovered on 100% (high) for 2 to 3 minutes, stirring the rice every minute until it is lightly browned. Follow the recipe as given.

The same procedure for browning rice can be used for Arroz Español, page 61, and for browning vermicelli in Sopa de Fideos, page 62.

As a child, I enjoyed my mother's Sopa de Fideos. I had sopa and a quesadilla for lunch. My adaptation is delicious and easy to prepare. Try pouring your favorite meat sauce over the sopa seca.

Arroz Español

Spanish Rice

Serve this traditional tasty rice with any Mexican dish.

Power level: high
Cooking time: 21 minutes
Servings: 6

1 (10-oz.) pkg. frozen peas and carrots

3 tablespoons vegetable oil

1/4 cup chopped onion

1 garlic clove, mashed

1/4 cup chopped bell pepper

2 cups uncooked quick-cooking rice

1 (14-1/2-oz.) can chicken broth

1 (8-oz.) can tomato sauce

1/2 teaspoon salt

1/2 teaspoon dried-leaf oregano, crushed

Place peas and carrots in a 1-1/2-quart casserole; cover and microwave on 100% (high) 9 minutes. Drain off liquid. Place peas and carrots in another dish; set aside.

Combine oil, onion, garlic and bell pepper in first casserole. Cover with waxed paper; microwave on 100% (high) 2 minutes. Stir in rice, peas and carrots, broth, tomato sauce, salt and oregano. Cover and microwave on 100% (high) 10 minutes. Let stand 5 minutes before serving.

Each serving contains:

Cal	Prot	Carb	Fib	Tot. Fat	Sat. Fat	Chol	Sodium
341	8g	60g	4g	8g	1g	0	227mg

I always thought that the addition of peas and carrots gives Spanish Rice a pretty color. I use quick-cooking rice to speed up the cooking.

Sopa de Fideos

Vermicelli

Sopa seca or dry soup, is pasta cooked in a broth until the liquid is absorbed.

Power level: high
Cooking time: 13 minutes
Servings: 6

1/4 cup chopped bell pepper

1 cup canned tomatoes

1/4 cup chopped onion

1 garlic clove, chopped

2 tablespoons vegetable oil

**4 oz. coiled vermicelli
(2-1/2 cups)**

**2-1/2 cups chicken broth or beef
broth**

1/2 teaspoon salt, if desired

Combine bell pepper, tomatoes, onion, garlic and oil in a 2-quart casserole. Cover with waxed paper; microwave on 100% (high) 3 minutes. Break vermicelli into pieces; stir vermicelli, broth and salt, if desired, into tomato mixture. If broth is salty, omit salt. Cover with waxed paper; microwave on 100% (high) 10 minutes, stirring after 5 minutes. Let stand 5 minutes before serving. Vermicelli should be tender but firm.

Each serving contains:

Cal	Prot	Carb	Fib	Tot. Fat	Sat. Fat	Chol	Sodium
95	3g	8g	1g	5g	0	0	66mg

Frijoles Puré

Puréed Beans

Tastes just like refried beans without frying. Either black or pinto beans can be used.

Power level: medium-high, high
Cooking time: 6 minutes
Servings: 4 (1/2-cup) servings

1 (16-oz.) can black or pinto beans, drained

1 garlic clove, mashed

1/2 teaspoon ground cumin

1/4 cup chopped onion

1 teaspoon red-chile powder

1/2 cup beef broth or 1/2 teaspoon instant beef-bouillon granules in 1/2 cup hot water

1/2 cup shredded cheese (2 oz.)

Salt to taste

Place all ingredients except cheese in a blender or food processor and blend until puréed. Put puréed bean mixture in a 1-1/2 quart casserole dish, add 1/4 cup cheese and salt to taste; blend well.

Cover with waxed paper and microwave on 70% (medium-high) 6 minutes, stirring after 3 minutes. Stir beans and top with remaining shredded cheese and microwave on 100% (high) 30 seconds or until cheese melts. Serve.

Each serving contains:

Cal	Prot	Carb	Fib	Tot. Fat	Sat. Fat	Chol	Sodium
216	14g	29g	11g	6g	3g	15mg	96mg

Arroz Verde

Green Rice

Bell pepper, fresh cilantro and serrano or jalapeño chiles give this dish a pleasing taste and its attractive green color.

Power level: high
Cooking time: 10 minutes
Servings: 5 to 6

1 tablespoon vegetable oil

1/4 cup chopped onion

1 garlic clove, chopped

1/4 cup chopped bell pepper

1 fresh serrano or jalapeño chile, finely chopped, if desired

2 cups uncooked quick-cooking rice

2 cups chicken broth or 2 chicken bouillon cubes dissolved in 2 cups hot water

1/2 teaspoon salt

1/4 cup chopped fresh cilantro or parsley

Combine oil, onion, garlic, bell pepper and chile, if desired, in a 2-quart casserole. Cover with waxed paper; microwave on 100% (high) 2 minutes. Stir rice, broth, salt and cilantro or parsley into onion mixture. Cover with waxed paper; microwave on 100% (high) 8 minutes. Let stand 5 minutes before serving.

Each serving contains:

Cal	Prot	Carb	Fib	Tot. Fat	Sat. Fat	Chol	Sodium
269	6g	52g	2g	3g	0	0	182mg

Comidas de Carne

Shredded cooked beef and pork are popular. They are simmered in an array of sauces. Two favorites are Machaca and Carne Adobada.

I prepare a *caldo* or soup with my meals. Caldos contain a variety of spices and are generally made with stock, either chicken or beef. To save time, I substitute beef or chicken bouillon, chicken consommé or beef broth instead of stock.

Sopa aguada or wet soup, is made with broth. Caldo de Cocido is clear, made with meat and vegetables.

Sopas, including Pozole or Albóndigas, have a flour or corn thickening base. These are complete meals. *Caldillo* or Mexican Stew is great for cold winter days. Diced potatoes add to the meal and are used as a filler in many dishes such as meat burritos and tacos.

The sound of sizzling meat and the aroma of a barbecue on an outside open fire concluded many weekend family-and-friend-get-togethers. Not only were there backyard gatherings, but it was exciting to meet along the banks of the Rio Grande for an open-pit barbecue.

Today I shorten the grilling time by partially cooking the meat in the microwave oven before barbecuing. In a covered casserole dish I microwave on 50% (medium) power until half-cooked. Then I take the meat outside and complete the barbecue—with Chile Barbecue Sauce of course!

Albóndigas

Meatball Soup

*Mint leaves give this main-dish soup
a distinctive flavor.*

Power level: high, medium-high
Cooking time: 22 minutes
Servings: 4

**1 lb. ground beef or ground
   turkey**

**3 tablespoons Taco Seasoning
   Mix, page 8, or 1 (1-1/4-oz.)
   pkg. taco seasoning mix**

**1/2 cup dry bread crumbs or 1/4
   cup oatmeal**

1 egg or 2 egg whites

**4 cups beef broth or 4 teaspoons
   instant beef-bouillon granules
   dissolved in 4 cups hot water**

2 tablespoons all-purpose flour

**2 teaspoons dried mint leaves or
   fresh cilantro leaves**

1/2 teaspoon salt

**1 teaspoon azafrán or saffron, if
   desired**

To dry fresh mint remove
leaves from stems; scatter 1/4
cup leaves on a paper napkin.
Microwave on 100% (high) 1 to
2 minutes or until dried.

Combine ground beef or turkey,
seasoning mix, bread crumbs and
egg in a bowl. Shape mixture into 24
meatballs. Place meatballs in a
microwave browning dish or 2-quart
casserole. Cover with waxed paper;
microwave on 100% (high) 3 minutes. Rearrange meatballs; cover and
microwave on 100% (high) another
3 minutes or until cooked through.
Drain off fat; set meatballs aside.

Combine broth and flour in a 2-
quart casserole; beat with a whisk
until smooth. Cover with waxed
paper; microwave on 100% (high)
6 minutes or until boiling.

Drop cooked meatballs into hot
broth along with mint or cilantro,
salt and azafrán or saffron. Cover,
microwave on 70% (medium-high)
10 minutes; stir after 5 minutes.
Serve hot.

Each serving contains:

Cal	Prot	Carb	Fib	Tot. Fat	Sat. Fat	Chol	Sodium
424	35g	17g	2g	24g	9g	153mg	748mg

Barbacoa de Costillas

Chile Barbecued Ribs

If you enjoy the great taste of barbecue, you will love these ribs.

Power level: medium or high
Cooking time: 70 minutes, or 25
    minutes in microwave
    pressure cooker
Servings: 4

3 lbs. pork or beef spareribs

1 cup Chile Barbecue Sauce, page 16

If using an open dish, separate individual spareribs. Place ribs, meaty side up, in a 12" x 8" flat-bottom casserole. Cover with waxed paper; microwave on 50% (medium) 40 minutes, rearrange ribs every 10 minutes. Drain fat. Pour sauce over ribs. Cover with waxed paper; microwave on 50% (medium) 30 minutes, rearrange ribs every 10 minutes. Let stand 5 minutes before serving.

For a microwave pressure cooker, place individual ribs in pressure cooker. Add 1/4 cup water. Close pressure cooker; put on pressure-regulator weight. Microwave on 100% (high) 10 minutes. Let pressure cooker stand with pressure 5 minutes. If pressure cooker has a pressure-indicating gauge or stem, standing time should be the time it takes for indicator to show pressure has dropped. Remove pressure regulator weight; open pressure cooker. Discard liquid. Pour barbecue sauce over ribs. To keep ribs from over-browning, place foil over ribs as described for covering tamales, page 31.

Close pressure cooker; put on pressure-regulator weight. Microwave on 100% (high) 15 minutes. Let pressure cooker stand with pressure 10 minutes. If pressure cooker has a pressure-indicating gauge or stem, standing time should be the time it takes for indicator to show pressure has dropped. Remove pressure-regulator weight; open pressure cooker. Serve ribs hot.

Each serving contains:

Cal	Prot	Carb	Fib	Tot. Fat	Sat. Fat	Chol	Sodium
663	43g	16g	2g	47g	17g	171mg	624mg

Caldillo

Mexican Stew

A delicious, thick, hearty stew; great served with warm tortillas.

Power level: medium, medium-high, high
Cooking time: 27 to 33 minutes
Servings: 4

1 lb. lean beef round steak, cut in 1-inch cubes

1/2 cup water

1 garlic clove, chopped

1/2 cup chopped onion

1/2 teaspoon whole cominos, crushed

1/2 teaspoon dried-leaf oregano, crushed

2 cups diced potatoes

1/4 cup diced green chiles

1/2 teaspoon salt

1/2 cup water

1-1/2 tablespoons all-purpose flour

Combine beef, 1/2 cup water, garlic, onion, cominos and oregano in a 2-quart casserole. Cover with waxed paper; microwave on 50% (medium) 10 minutes. Add potatoes, chiles and salt. Cover and microwave on 70% (medium-high) 15 to 20 minutes, stirring after 8 minutes.

Combine 1/2 cup water and flour in a small bowl, stirring until smooth. Stir into meat mixture. Cover and microwave on 100% (high) 2 to 3 minutes or until tender; stir mixture. Let stand 5 minutes before serving.

Each serving contains:

Cal	Prot	Carb	Fib	Tot. Fat	Sat. Fat	Chol	Sodium
247	26g	19g	2g	7g	3g	70mg	325mg

Caldo de Cocido

Vegetable Beef Soup

Have your butcher cut the beef short ribs in half.

Power level: high, medium,
    medium-high
Cooking time: 58 to 63 minutes
Servings: 4 to 6

1 cup uncooked quick-cooking rice

1 cup water

1/2 teaspoon salt

2-1/2 lbs. beef short ribs, cut in half

1/4 cup chopped onion

1/4 cup chopped bell pepper

1 garlic clove, chopped

1/2 teaspoon dried-leaf oregano

5 cups water

1/4 cup chopped green chiles

4 medium carrots, thinly sliced

2 cups thinly sliced zucchini

1/2 teaspoon salt, if desired

1 tablespoon chopped fresh cilantro

Combine rice, 1 cup water and 1/2 teaspoon salt in a 1-1/2-quart casserole. Cover, microwave on 100% (high) 8 minutes or until tender; set rice aside.

Place short ribs, onion, bell pepper, garlic and oregano in a 3-quart casserole. Cover with a lid; microwave on 50% (medium) 20 minutes. Add 5 cups water, chiles, carrots, zucchini and salt.

Cover and microwave on 70% (medium-high) 30 to 35 minutes or until tender, stirring after 15 minutes. Stir in cooked rice; garnish with cilantro. Serve hot.

Each serving contains:

Cal	Prot	Carb	Fib	Tot. Fat	Sat. Fat	Chol	Sodium
330	24g	33g	3g	11g	4g	61mg	254mg

Caldo de Cocido #2

Vegetable Beef Soup

This version uses the microwave pressure cooker.

Power level: high
Cooking time: 33 minutes
Servings: 4 to 5

1 cup uncooked quick-cooking rice

1 cup water

1/2 teaspoon salt

1-1/2 lbs. beef short ribs, cut in half

1/4 cup chopped onion

1/4 cup chopped bell pepper

1 garlic clove, minced

1/2 teaspoon dried-leaf oregano

1/4 cup chopped green chiles

2-1/2 cups water

2 medium carrots, thinly sliced

1 cup thinly sliced zucchini

1/2 teaspoon salt, if desired

1 tablespoon chopped fresh cilantro

Combine rice, 1 cup water and 1/2 teaspoon salt in a 1-1/2-quart casserole. Cover and microwave on 100% (high) 8 minutes or until rice is tender: set rice aside.

Place short ribs, onion, bell pepper, garlic, oregano, chiles, 2-1/2 cups water, carrots and zucchini in a microwave pressure cooker. Close pressure cooker; put on pressure-regulator weight.

Microwave on 100% (high) 25 minutes. Let pressure cooker stand with pressure 10 minutes. If pressure cooker has a pressure-indicating gauge or stem, standing time should be the time it takes for indicator to show pressure has dropped. Remove pressure-regulator weight; open pressure cooker. Stir in cooked rice and salt, garnish with cilantro. Serve hot.

Each serving contains:

Cal	Prot	Carb	Fib	Tot. Fat	Sat. Fat	Chol	Sodium
271	16g	36g	2g	7g	3g	36mg	260mg

Carne Adobada

Marinated Meat

Adobada is a thick sauce made with red-chile sauce, vinegar and spices. Meat was prepared in this manner as a means of preserving it. Serve this tasty combination rolled inside warm tortillas.

Power level: medium
Cooking time: 50 minutes
Servings: 5

2 lbs. sliced pork roast, about 1/2-inch thick

2 cups cooked Chile Colorado, page 10

1/4 cup vinegar

1 tablespoon vegetable oil

1 garlic clove, chopped

3 whole cloves

Place sliced pork in a large, flat-bottom casserole. Combine Chile Colorado, vinegar, oil, garlic and cloves in a separate dish; pour mixture over pork slices. Cover and refrigerate overnight.

Remove whole cloves from pork. Cover with a lid; microwave on 50% (medium) 50 minutes, rearranging meat every 10 minutes. Pork should be tender. If not, cover and microwave on 50% (medium) another 10 minutes. Let stand 5 minutes before serving.

Each serving contains:

Cal	Prot	Carb	Fib	Tot. Fat	Sat Fat	Chol	Sodium
362	42g	11g	2g	17g	5g	100mg	210mg

Carne con Chile Colorado

Red Chile Meat

Simmering the meat in red-chile sauce enhances its flavor.

Power level: medium, medium-high
Cooking time: 35 minutes
Servings: 4 to 5

1 lb. lean pork or beef, cut in 1-inch cubes

1 garlic clove, mashed

1/8 teaspoon whole cominos, crushed

1/8 teaspoon cilantro seeds, crushed

1/8 teaspoon dried-leaf oregano, crushed

1/2 teaspoon salt

Garnish:
2 cups uncooked Chile Colorado, page 10

1 tablespoon all-purpose flour

Place meat in a 1-1/2-quart casserole. Cover with a lid; microwave on 50% (medium) 15 minutes. Stir in garlic, cominos, cilantro, oregano and salt; set mixture aside.

Combine Chile Colorado and flour in a small bowl; pour mixture over meat mixture. Cover with a lid or waxed paper; microwave on 70% (medium-high) 20 minutes or until tender, stirring after 10 minutes. Serve hot.

Each serving contains:

Cal	Prot	Carb	Fib	Tot. Fat	Sat. Fat	Chol	Sodium
197	22g	12g	2g	7g	2g	50mg	383mg

Photo back cover

Carne con Verduras

Meat with Vegetables

Spicy seasonings are added to these vegetables and meat to give this dish a zesty flavor. Great dish served with steamed rice.

Power level: medium, medium-high
Cooking time: 30 to 35 minutes
Servings: 4

1 lb. beef round steak, cut in 1-inch cubes

1/2 cup water

1/3 cup chopped onion

1/3 cup chopped bell pepper

1 cup diced zucchini

1 (10-oz.) pkg. frozen whole-kernel corn

1 tomato, chopped

1/4 cup diced green chiles

1 garlic clove, chopped

1/2 teaspoon dried-leaf oregano, crushed

1/2 teaspoon salt

Combine beef and water in a 2-quart casserole. Cover with lid; microwave on 50% (medium) 10 minutes. Add remaining ingredients; cover and microwave on 70% (medium-high) 20 to 25 minutes or until tender, stirring after 10 minutes. Serve hot.

Each serving contains:

Cal	Prot	Carb	Fib	Tot. Fat	Sat. Fat	Chol	Sodium
247	28g	20g	4g	7g	3g	70mg	329mg

❦ **Variation**
Add 2 cups of cooked pinto beans and 2 chopped green onions during final cooking period.

Photo on back cover

Chile con Carne

Chile with Meat

Serve this favorite with warm flour tortillas.

Power level: high, medium-high, medium
Cooking time: 38 minutes
Servings: 6

1/2 cup chopped onion

1/2 cup chopped bell pepper

1 garlic clove, chopped

1 tablespoon vegetable oil

1 lb. beef sirloin or top round, cut in 1-inch cubes

1 (16-oz.) can stewed tomatoes

2 (15-oz.) cans pinto beans

3 tablespoons red-chile powder

2 tablespoons all-purpose flour

1 teaspoon salt

1/4 teaspoon whole cominos, crushed

1/4 teaspoon dried-leaf oregano, crushed

Garnish:
1 cup shredded lettuce, if desired

1 cup shredded Cheddar cheese (4 oz.), if desired

Combine onion, bell pepper, garlic and oil in a 1-1/2-quart casserole. Cover with waxed paper; microwave on 100% (high) 3 minutes. Set aside.

Place beef in a 2-1/2-quart casserole. Cover and microwave on 50% (medium) 10 minutes. Drain beef, reserving drippings. Add 1/2 cup beef drippings, cooked vegetables and remaining ingredients (except lettuce and cheese) to cooked beef; stir to combine.

Cover and microwave on 70% (medium-high) 25 minutes or until tender, stirring after 12 minutes. Let stand 5 minutes. Garnish with shredded lettuce and cheese. Serve hot.

Each serving contains:

Cal	Prot	Carb	Fib	Tot. Fat	Sat. Fat	Chol	Sodium
253	23g	24g	9g	8g	2g	47mg	554mg

Chorizo

Seasoned Sausage

Chorizo goes great with Huevos Revueltos, scrambled eggs, page 56.

Power level: high
Cooking time: 4 to 6 minutes
Servings: 5 to 6

1/4 teaspoon coriander seed

1/2 teaspoon whole cominos

1 teaspoon dried-leaf oregano

3 garlic cloves

1 lb. fresh bulk pork sausage

2 tablespoons red-chile powder

1 teaspoon salt

1 teaspoon paprika

3 tablespoons white vinegar

Use a molcajete, or mortar and pestle to prepare spices. If unavailable, use a fork and a small plate to crush spices. Crush together coriander, cominos, oregano and garlic. Add crushed spices to sausage along with chile powder, salt and paprika. Thoroughly blend sausage and seasonings. Add vinegar; blend well. Refrigerate 24 to 48 hours.

Crumble chorizo in a 2-quart casserole. Cover with waxed paper; microwave on 100% (high) 4 to 6 minutes, stir after 3 minutes. Sausage is cooked when no longer pink. If additional cooking is needed, cover and microwave on 100% (high) 1 minute or until cooked. Drain fat. Serve hot.

Each serving contains:

Cal	Prot	Carb	Fib	Tot. Fat	Sat. Fat	Chol	Sodium
329	9g	3g	1g	31g	11g	52mg	885mg

❦ **Variation**
Turkey Chorizo
Substitute turkey for pork sausage.

Chuletas de Puerco en Chile

Chile Pork Chops

An extremely easy way to prepare tasty pork chops.

Power level: medium-high
Cooking time: 24 minutes
Servings: 4

3 tablespoons Taco Seasoning Mix, page 8, or 1 (1-1/4-oz.) pkg. taco seasoning mix

3 tablespoons all-purpose flour

4 pork chops

Shake seasoning mix and flour in a plastic bag. Place each pork chop into bag, shaking to coat with mixture. Place seasoned chops in a microwave browning dish or 2-quart casserole. Cover with waxed paper; microwave on 70% (medium-high) 12 minutes.

Turn chops over and rotate dish; microwave on 70% (medium-high) 12 minutes or until chops are done. Let stand 5 minutes before serving. Serve hot.

Each serving contains:

Cal	Prot	Carb	Fib	Tot. Fat	Sat. Fat	Chol	Sodium
207	24g	9g	1g	8g	3g	71mg	343mg

Chuletas de Puerco en Mole Verde

Pork Chops in Green-Chile Sauce

Delight friends and family with this unusual combination. The sauce gives the pork a spicy, nutty taste.

Power level: medium-high
Cooking time: 24 minutes
Servings: 4

4 pork chops

1-1/2 cups Mole Verde, page 18

Simmering the Mole Verde on 50% (medium) 20 minutes before pouring it over the pork chops enhances the flavor of this dish. Mole Verde can also be poured over cooked, shredded pork and served rolled in a warm tortilla.

Place pork chops in a flat-bottom casserole. Cover with waxed paper; microwave on 70% (medium-high) 4 minutes. Turn chops over and rotate dish. Cover with waxed paper; microwave on 70% (medium-high) 4 minutes. Drain off any fat.

Pour Mole Verde over chops. Cover with waxed paper; microwave on 70% (medium-high) 16 minutes, rotating dish after 8 minutes. Chops should be done. If not, cover and microwave on 70% (medium-high) 2 minutes or until chops are done. Serve hot.

Each serving contains:

Cal	Prot	Carb	Fib	Tot. Fat	Sat. Fat	Chol	Sodium
260	27g	5g	2g	14g	3g	71mg	127mg

Fajitas

Little Thin Belts

Substitute chicken or pork tenderloin for beef.

Power level: high, medium
Cooking time: 10 to 11 minutes
Servings: 4 to 5

1 lb. beef skirt steak, flank steak or top round steak

1/2 teaspoon whole cominos, crushed

1/4 teaspoon dried-leaf oregano, crushed

3 garlic cloves, mashed

1/4 cup water

1 teaspoon white pepper

1 teaspoon black pepper

1 teaspoon paprika

1 tablespoon lemon juice

1 teaspoon onion powder

1 teaspoon garlic powder

1-1/2 cups chopped tomatoes

1 cup chopped bell pepper

1-1/2 cups chopped onion

1 tablespoon vegetable oil

4 to 5 (8-inch) flour tortillas

Pound meat on both sides. Slice across grain in 1/4-inch-thick lengthwise strips. Combine all ingredients except oil and tortillas in a large bowl. Marinate at least 1 hour, turn mixture after 30 minutes.

Heat a microwave browning dish at 100% (high) 4 minutes. Use hot pads to remove dish from oven. Drain meat, reserve marinade and vegetables. Place half the meat in hot browning dish. Cover with waxed paper; microwave on 50% (medium) 4 to 5 minutes, rearrange after 2 minutes. Repeat with remaining meat. Set aside.

Place 1 tablespoon oil in a 2-quart casserole; add vegetables and marinade. Cover with waxed paper; microwave on 100% (high) 6 minutes, stirring after 3 minutes. Add meat. Serve hot with flour tortillas.

Each serving contains:

Cal	Prot	Carb	Fib	Tot. Fat	Sat. Fat	Chol	Sodium
314	23g	30g	3g	13g	4g	45mg	208mg

❦   ❦   ❦

Fajitas have been a traditional Mexican food in the cattle country along the Mexican border. These marinated steak strips are traditionally eaten rolled in a warm flour tortilla, topped with salsa, shredded cheese and shredded lettuce.

I suppose you can say that Fajitas are a rebirth of an old idea. Originally, they were made from the tough beef skirt steak which was tenderized by pounding and marinating the beef strips in lemon or lime juice with spices added.

My mother recalls her grandmother telling her that when she worked on a ranch near the Organ Mountains in Southern New Mexico, she prepared meals in the bunk house. Every piece of meat was used including the skirt steak. She would guisar *or stir-fry the marinated meat. She usually prepared the meat in an* olla *or large cast-iron pot, which was too heavy for her to lift. Ranch hands would lift the pot for her.*

Blue baked-enamel cookware was often used in place of the cast-iron because it was lighter and less expensive. I remember the neighborhood women buying it from my great-aunt Lupe's store. She always had a variety of baked-enamel cookware.

In preparing a browning dish for Fajitas, follow manufacturer's directions for heating. Although I recommend heating a browning dish 4 minutes before placing the tenderized meat strips in it, you should not heat the dish longer than recommended by the manufacturer. My recipe for Fajitas is easy to prepare and I recommend you try it!

Machaca

Shredded Beef

Machaca is an excellent filling for burritos. It is also delicious when added to frijoles.

Power level: medium, medium-high
Cooking time: 95 to 105 minutes
Servings: 6 to 8

2-1/2 lbs. boneless beef

1/4 teaspoon whole black peppercorns, crushed

1/4 teaspoon cilantro seed, crushed

2 garlic cloves, mashed

1/2 cup sliced onion

1/2 cup water

1/4 teaspoon whole cominos, crushed

1/2 teaspoon dried-leaf oregano, crushed

1/2 teaspoon salt

1/4 cup diced green chiles

1 (8-oz.) can stewed tomatoes

Rub beef with peppercorns, cilantro and garlic; place in 2-quart casserole. Add onion, water. Cover with lid; microwave on 50% (medium) 25 minutes per pound. Meat is done when no longer pink. If not done, cover and microwave on 50% (medium) 5 to 10 minutes. Place beef on cutting board. Reserve drippings.

When beef is cooled, pull it apart with a fork or cut meat into strips. Place meat, cominos, oregano, salt, chiles, tomatoes and 2/3 cup reserved drippings in 2-quart casserole. Cover and microwave on 70% (medium-high) 15 minutes, stirring after 7-1/2 minutes. Season to taste.

Each serving contains:

Cal	Prot	Carb	Fib	Tot. Fat	Sat. Fat	Chol	Sodium
255	37g	3g	1g	10g	4g	104mg	263mg

Ingredients can be cooked in a microwave pressure cooker.

Diablitas

Little She-Devils

My mother's recipe. Red-chile sauce poured over spicy meatballs describes the appearance and taste of this food. But why "She-Devils" you may ask?

Power level: high, medium-high
Cooking time: 22 minutes
Servings: 4

**1 lb. ground turkey or
     ground pork**

1 garlic clove, chopped

1/2 cup chopped onion

1 teaspoon salt

**1/2 teaspoon whole cominos,
     crushed**

**1/2 teaspoon dried-leaf oregano,
     crushed**

1 egg or 2 egg whites

**2 cups cooked Chile Colorado,
     page 10**

Combine turkey or pork, garlic, onion, salt, cominos, oregano and egg or egg whites in a large bowl. Shape pork mixture into 24 meatballs, placing meatballs in a microwave browning dish or flat-bottom casserole. Cover with waxed paper; microwave on 100% (high) 4 minutes.

Rearrange meatballs, place those that were on the outer edge in the center and those from the center around the edge. Cover and microwave on 100% (high) 4 minutes. Drain off fat; place meatballs in a 2-quart casserole.

Pour Chile Colorado over meatballs. Cover and microwave on 70% (medium-high) 14 minutes, stirring after 7 minutes. Serve hot.

Each serving contains:

Cal	Prot	Carb	Fib	Tot. Fat	Sat. Fat	Chol	Sodium
310	29g	15g	3g	15g	4g	122mg	792mg

Pozole

Meat & Hominy Soup

A wonderful dish for Christmas Eve or any cold night.

Power level: high, medium-high
Cooking time: 30 minutes
Servings: 6

2 cups diced cooked beef or pork

1 (1-lb.,13-oz.) can white hominy, drained

4 cups water

2 cups cooked Chile Colorado, page 10

1 teaspoon dried-leaf oregano, crushed

Salt to taste

Chopped onions, if desired

Crushed oregano, if desired

Combine beef or pork, hominy, water, Chile Colorado, and oregano in a deep, 3-quart casserole. Cover with waxed paper; microwave on 100% (high)20 minutes or until mixture begins to boil.

Stir well; cover and microwave on 70% (medium-high) 10 minutes, stirring after 5 minutes. Pour soup into serving bowls. Salt to taste and sprinkle with onions and oregano, if desired.

Each serving contains:

Cal	Prot	Carb	Fib	Tot. Fat	Sat. Fat	Chol	Sodium
204	16g	27g	4g	4g	1g	36mg	127mg

🐃   🐃   🐃

Instead of a menudo recipe, I've included a recipe for pozole. They are similar soups; menudo is made with tripe and pozole is made with beef or pork.

Torta de Carne Molida

Chile Meatloaf

Meatloaf becomes a special treat served hot or cold.

Power level: medium-high
Cooking time: 20 minutes
Servings: 6

1 (8-oz.) can tomato sauce

1-1/2 lbs. ground beef or ground turkey

1 cup fresh bread crumbs

1/4 cup chopped onion

1/4 cup chopped bell pepper

1 garlic clove, chopped

1 egg or 2 egg whites

3 tablespoons Taco Seasoning Mix, page 8, or 1 (1-1/4-oz.) pkg. taco seasoning mix

1/4 cup diced green chiles

Set half the tomato sauce aside. In a large bowl, combine remaining tomato sauce and all other ingredients; blend well.

Grease or spray with vegetable cooking spray a microwave-safe ring mold or a round, glass cake dish. Place an inverted custard cup in center of cake dish. Pat meat mixture into greased mold or dish. Pour remaining tomato sauce over top of meat mixture.

Cover with waxed paper; microwave on 70% (medium-high) 20 minutes, rotating dish after 10 minutes. Let stand 5 minutes. If meat is still pink, cover and microwave on 70% (medium-high) 1 minute or until cooked through. Serve hot.

Each serving contains:

Cal	Prot	Carb	Fib	Tot. Fat	Sat. Fat	Chol	Sodium
371	31g	11g	2g	23g	9g	134mg	556mg

Comidas de Pollo y Pescado

In my chicken dishes, I use *mole* (chocolate-peanut) or *pipián* (pumpkin seed) sauces.

Baking a whole chicken in the microwave, boning and freezing it in 2-cup portions works great. You always have chicken for those "What can I prepare?" days. Tacos, enchiladas and various casseroles use cooked chicken as well as some of my soup recipes. Caldo de Pollo is a chicken soup containing vegetables and rice. Caldo Azteca is a chicken broth soup with pieces of chicken. Caldo de Queso is a delicious creamy soup made with chicken broth, milk and cheese.

Although there is a variety of fish dishes in Mexican cuisine, most are identified with the coastal areas of Mexico. My recipes use fish that are available in most markets.

I remember that my mother always made it a point to use only fresh thin fish fillets without the *espinas* or bones, because like most kids, we did not like to be bothered with removing the bones.

Azafrán (Mexican saffron) is a plentiful spice used in cooking. It's made from deep-crimson stigmas of the Mexican saffron crocus. Note that this is a different crocus than is used in Spanish or Turkish saffron. Azafrán gives the dish an attractive crimson-flecked color and distinctive taste.

Pechuga de Pollo con Queso

Chicken Breasts with Cheese

Chicken topped with melted cheese.

Power level: high, medium-high
Cooking time: 9 minutes
Servings: 6

1 tablespoon vegetable oil or chicken broth

1/2 cup chopped onion

1 garlic clove, chopped

2 tablespoons cilantro leaves

1/4 cup chopped green chiles or 1 (4-oz.) can diced green chiles

2 tablespoons chopped red bell pepper, if desired

1 lb. cooked boneless chicken breast, cut in strips

4 (10-inch) flour tortillas

3/4 cup shredded Monterey Jack or mozzarella cheese (3 oz.)

Salsa de Cominos, page 6, or PACE®Picante Sauce

Combine oil or chicken broth, onion, garlic, cilantro, green chiles and red bell pepper, if desired, in a 1-1/2-quart casserole dish. Cover with waxed paper and microwave on 100% (high) 3 minutes, stirring after 1-1/2 minutes. Add chicken strips and mix well. Set aside.

To heat tortillas, see page 34, paragraph 2. Cut into 6 wedges and separate so they won't stick together.

Lightly grease or spray with vegetable cooking spray a 12" x 8" flat-bottom casserole dish. Starting from the bottom of the tortilla wedge, place a chicken strip on the tortilla. Top with 1 teaspoon cheese. Roll up filled tortilla. Place rolled tortilla wedges in dish, cover with waxed paper and microwave on 70% (medium-high) 5 minutes, turning dish after 2-1/2 minutes, or until chicken is heated. Serve ·with Salsa de Cominos or PACE® Picante Sauce.

Each serving contains:

Cal	Prot	Carb	Fib	Tot. Fat	Sat. Fat	Chol	Sodium
308	28g	23g	1g	12g	4g	71mg	267mg

Arroz con Pollo

Chicken with Rice

Great taste and eye appeal.

Power level: high, medium-high
Cooking time: 45 to 50 minutes
Servings: 6

Browning Mix:
1 teaspoon paprika

2 tablespoons brown sugar

1/2 teaspoon poultry seasoning

1/4 teaspoon garlic salt or
   regular salt

1/2 teaspoon onion powder

Chicken:
1 (10-oz.) pkg. frozen peas and
   carrots

1 (3-1/2-lb.) chicken, cut up

1 tablespoon vegetable oil

1/2 cup chopped onion

1/2 cup chopped bell pepper

1 garlic clove

2 cups uncooked quick-cooking
   rice

1/2 teaspoon salt

1 (8-oz.) can stewed tomatoes

1-1/2 teaspoons azafrán or
   saffron

For browning mix, combine all ingredients. Store in an airtight container for future use.

Place peas and carrots in a 1-1/2-quart casserole. Cover with waxed paper; microwave on 100% (high) 10 minutes. Set vegetables aside.

Coat chicken pieces with browning mix; place coated pieces in a 2-1/2-quart casserole. Cover; microwave on 100% (high) 20 to 25 minutes, rearranging chicken after 12 minutes. Pour drippings into a measuring cup; set aside. Remove chicken.

Combine oil, onion, bell pepper and garlic in same casserole. Cover; microwave on 100% (high) 3 minutes. Add water to drippings to make 2 cups. Add drippings, rice, salt, tomatoes and azafrán or saffron to onion mixture. Cover; microwave on 70% (medium-high) 7 minutes. Add chicken, peas and carrots. Cover and microwave on 70% (medium-high) 5 minutes. Serve hot.

Each serving contains:

Cal	Prot	Carb	Fib	Tot. Fat	Sat Fat	Chol	Sodium
623	63g	64g	4g	11g	2g	186mg	576mg

Barbacoa de Pollo

Chile Barbecued Chicken

Spicy barbecue sauce goes well with the flavor of chicken.

Power level: high
Cooking time: 20 to 25 minutes
Servings: 4 to 6

1 (3-lb.) frying chicken, cut up

1 cup Chile Barbecue Sauce, page 16

Place chicken in a 2-1/2-quart casserole. Pour sauce over chicken. Cover with waxed paper; microwave on 100% (high) 20 to 25 minutes, turning dish and rearranging chicken every 10 minutes or until cooked through. Let stand 5 minutes before serving.

Each serving contains:

Cal	Prot	Carb	Fib	Tot. Fat	Sat. Fat	Chol	Sodium
202	26g	11g	2g	6g	1g	80mg	416mg

Cacerola de Pollo

Chicken Casserole

Sour cream enhances the taste of this complete meal in a casserole.

Power level: high, medium-high
Cooking time: 15 to 17 minutes
Servings: 6

1 tablespoon vegetable oil

1/4 cup chopped bell pepper

1/2 cup chopped onion

1 garlic clove, chopped

1/8 teaspoon whole cominos, crushed

1/4 cup chopped green chiles

1 cup plus 2 tablespoons beef broth

3 tablespoons all-purpose flour

1 egg or 2 egg whites

1 cup dairy sour cream

2 cups diced cooked chicken

6 cups salt-free tortilla chips (6 oz.)

1 cup shredded Cheddar cheese (4 oz.)

1/2 cup sliced ripe olives or 1 (2-1/4-oz.) can sliced ripe olives

Combine oil, bell pepper, onion, garlic and cominos in a 1-1/2-quart casserole. Cover with waxed paper; microwave on 100% (high) 2 minutes. Add chiles, broth and flour; blend. Cover with waxed paper; microwave 3 minutes more, stirring after 1-1/2 minutes. Beat egg or egg whites; stir egg, sour cream and chicken into mixture. Set aside.

Grease or spray with vegetable cooking spray a 12" x 8" casserole. Reserve 15 tortilla chips and 1/3 cup cheese. Line casserole with tortilla chips. Top with 1/3 chicken mixture and 1/3 remaining cheese and olives. Repeat with two additional layers. Cover with waxed paper; microwave on 70% (medium-high) 10 to 12 minutes, rotating after 5 minutes. Sprinkle with reserved cheese. Cover and microwave on 100% (high) 30 seconds.

Place remaining chips around edge of dish. Let stand 5 minutes.

Each serving contains:

Cal	Prot	Carb	Fib	Tot. Fat	Sat. Fat	Chol	Sodium
679	29g	60g	11g	38g	12g	111mg	278mg

Chile Verde con Pollo

Green Chile with Chicken

A variation of the enchilada.

Power level: high, medium-high
Cooking time: 21 minutes
Servings: 6

1/2 cup chopped onion

1/2 cup chopped bell pepper

1 garlic clove, chopped

1 tablespoon vegetable oil

1/2 cup diced green chiles

1/4 teaspoon paprika

1/4 teaspoon cumin

**1 cup chicken broth or
   1 teaspoon instant chicken
   bouillon granules dissolved in
   1 cup hot water**

1 cup dairy sour cream

**1/4 cup evaporated skimmed
   milk**

3 tablespoons flour

**1 cup shredded Cheddar cheese
   (4 oz.)**

**12 (6-inch) corn tortillas, cut in
   3/4-inch strips**

2 cups diced cooked chicken

Combine onion, bell pepper, garlic and oil in a 2-quart casserole. Cover with waxed paper; microwave on 100% (high) 4 minutes, stirring after 2 minutes. Add chiles, paprika, cumin, broth, sour cream, evaporated milk and flour. Blend mixture and set aside.

Grease or spray with vegetable cooking spray a 2-quart casserole. Set 1/4 cup cheese aside. With remaining cheese, alternate layers of tortilla, chicken, cheese and chicken sauce. Continue alternating layers until all ingredients are used, finishing with chicken sauce.

Cover with waxed paper; microwave on 70% (medium-high) 15 minutes, turning dish after 7-1/2 minutes. Sprinkle with reserved 1/4 cup cheese. Cover with waxed paper; microwave on 70% (medium-high) 2 minutes. Let stand 5 minutes.

Each serving contains:

Cal	Prot	Carb	Fib	Tot. Fat	Sat. Fat	Chol	Sodium
434	25g	35g	5g	22g	10g	76mg	186mg

Pollo Borracho

Drunken Chicken

Pollo Borracho has always been a favorite in my family. My daughter is always asking me to prepare it for her. I use cooking sherry, but you can also use flat beer.

Power level: medium-high, high
Cooking time: 38 to 43 minutes
Servings: 6

1/4 cup chopped onion

1 garlic clove, chopped

1/2 teaspoon dried-leaf oregano, crushed

1 (8-oz.) can tomato sauce

1/4 cup water

1/2 cup cooking sherry or flat beer

3 tablespoons Taco Seasoning Mix, page 8, or 1 (1-1/4-oz.) pkg. taco seasoning mix

3 tablespoons all-purpose flour

1 (3-lb.) frying chicken, cut up, skinned

Combine onion, garlic and oregano in a 2-1/2-quart casserole. Stir in tomato sauce and water. Cover with waxed paper; microwave on 70% (medium-high) 5 minutes. Pour tomato mixture into bowl. After tomato mixture cools, add sherry or beer; set aside.

Combine seasoning mix and flour in plastic bag; add chicken. Shaking bag gently, coat chicken with seasoning. Place chicken pieces in 2-1/2-quart casserole. Cover with waxed paper; microwave on 100% (high) 18 minutes; rearrange pieces and turn dish after 9 minutes. Pour off excess drippings. Pour tomato mixture over chicken. Cover with waxed paper; microwave on 70% (medium-high) 15 to 20 minutes or until chicken and sauce are bubbly hot. Serve immediately.

Each serving contains:

Cal	Prot	Carb	Fib	Tot. Fat	Sat. Fat	Chol	Sodium
201	26g	10g	1g	4g	1g	80mg	510mg

Rellenos de Pavo

Turkey Rellenos

The mild taste of ground turkey is enhanced by fresh mature red chile.

Power level: high
Cooking time: 8 to 9 minutes
Servings: 3

1/2 lb. ground turkey

1/4 teaspoon salt

1/4 teaspoon garlic powder

1/2 teaspoon onion powder

1/2 teaspoon dried-leaf oregano, crushed

6 fresh red or green chiles, roasted, page 3, or 1 (8-oz.) can whole roasted green chiles

1 cup shredded Cheddar cheese (4 oz.)

4 egg whites

1/4 teaspoon cream of tartar

1 tablespoon cornstarch or flour

1/2 teaspoon baking powder

1/8 teaspoon salt

1/4 teaspoon paprika

1 tablespoon vegetable oil

Place turkey in a 2-quart casserole. Cover with waxed paper; microwave on 100% (high) 3 minutes, stirring after 1-1/2 minutes. Let stand 5 minutes. Drain turkey, discard liquid. Stir in salt, garlic powder, onion powder and oregano; set aside.

Roast and peel fresh chiles, or use canned whole roasted chiles. Cut a lengthwise slit along each chile pod; remove seeds.

Reserve 1/2 cup cheese for topping. Using remaining cheese, fill each chile with 2 tablespoons turkey mixture and 1 tablespoon cheese; set stuffed chiles aside.

Beat egg whites until stiff, gradually add cream of tartar. Stir together cornstarch or flour, baking powder, salt and paprika and fold into beaten egg whites. Pour batter into a shallow glass pie plate; set aside.

Spread oil evenly in a 12" x 8" casserole. Dip each chile into batter, then place in casserole in one layer. Cover with waxed paper; microwave on 100% (high) 2 minutes. Turn chiles over. Cover and

microwave on 100% (high) 2 minutes. If batter is not cooked, microwave on 100% (high) 1 minute or
until done. Sprinkle reserved cheese
over rellenos. Cover with waxed
paper; microwave on 100% (high)
45 seconds. Serve hot.

Each serving contains:

Cal	Prot	Carb	Fib	Tot. Fat	Sat. Fat	Chol	Sodium
434	34g	12g	2g	28g	11g	92mg	698mg

❦ Variation
Substitute 1/2 lb. Turkey Chorizo,
page 75, for 1/2 lb. ground turkey.
Omit 1/4 teaspoon salt, garlic powder, onion powder and dried-leaf
oregano. Cook Turkey Chorizo
according to recipe directions for
Turkey Chorizo.

Pavo is Spanish for turkey
meat, but the live bird is called
guajolote. Cocono is a collo-
quial term for turkey that is
used locally in New Mexico.

Fresh red chiles are actually
green chiles that have been
allowed to ripen on the vine.
They are seasonal and are usually available in early autumn.
If you cannot find fresh red
chiles, substitute whole roasted
green chiles, fresh or canned.

Picadillo

Picadillo is a sweetened Mexican meat filling that is great in tacos or rolled in a flour tortilla.

Power level: medium-high
Cooking time: 4 minutes
Servings: 8 tacos

2 cups cooked, shredded turkey, chicken or beef

1 cup chopped tomatoes or 1 (14-1/2-oz.) can whole peeled tomatoes, drained, chopped

2 tablespoons chopped onion

1 garlic clove, finely chopped

2 tablespoons chopped cilantro

1/4 cup raisins

1/4 cup chopped pecans

1/4 teaspoon ground cloves

1 jalapeño chile, finely chopped, or 1 tablespoon canned jalapeño chile

8 corn or flour tortillas

Put cooked meat in a 1-1/2 quart casserole dish, set aside. Put tomatoes, onion, garlic, cilantro, raisins, pecans, cloves, and chopped jalapeño in a bowl and blend well. Pour picadillo mixture over cooked meat. Cover with waxed paper and microwave on 70% (medium-high) 4 minutes stirring after 2 minutes. Serve with corn or flour tortillas.

Each serving contains:

Cal	Prot	Carb	Fib	Tot. Fat	Sat. Fat	Chol	Sodium
172	13g	19g	3g	5g	1g	27mg	29mg

Pollo en Pipián

Chicken in Pumpkin-seed Sauce

Lowly pumpkin seeds add distinction to this chicken.

Power level: medium-high
Cooking time: 35 minutes
Servings: 4

1/2 cup shelled pumpkin seeds

**3 cups chicken broth or
3 chicken bouillon cubes
dissolved in 3 cups hot water**

3 tablespoons vegetable oil

3 tablespoons all-purpose flour

1 teaspoon coriander seeds

2 tablespoons red-chile powder

**3 tablespoons Taco Seasoning
Mix, page 8, or 1 (1-1/4-oz.)
pkg. taco seasoning mix**

1/4 cup sesame seeds

3 cups diced cooked chicken

If pumpkin seeds are salted, rinse in water; drain well. Combine pumpkin seeds, broth, oil, flour, coriander, chile powder, seasoning mix and sesame seeds in a blender; process until liquified. Pour mixture into a 1-1/2-quart casserole. Cover with waxed paper; microwave on 70% (medium-high) 15 minutes, stirring after 7-1/2 minutes. Add chicken to hot sauce; stir to blend. Cover with waxed paper; microwave on 70% (medium-high) 20 minutes, stirring after 10 minutes. Let stand 5 minutes. Serve hot.

Each serving contains:

Cal	Prot	Carb	Fib	Tot. Fat	Sat. Fat	Chol	Sodium
450	38g	17g	6g	26g	4g	88mg	404mg

Photo back cover

Caldo Azteca

Aztec Soup

Serve this chicken soup year 'round.

Power level: high, medium-high
Cooking time: 33 minutes
Servings: 4

1 tablespoon vegetable oil

1 garlic clove, chopped

1/2 cup chopped onion

1/2 cup chopped celery

1 cup diced cooked chicken

2 cups chicken broth

1 (28 oz.) can whole tomatoes, chopped

1/2 teaspoon poultry seasoning

3 tablespoons diced green chiles

1/2 teaspoon salt

1 cup thinly sliced carrots

3 tablespoons masa harina

1 cup water

Lime, sliced for garnish

Nonfat yogurt for garnish

Combine oil, garlic, onion, celery, and chicken in a 2-quart casserole. Cover with waxed paper; microwave on 100% (high) 3 minutes. Stir in chicken broth, tomatoes, poultry seasoning, chiles, salt and carrots. Cover with waxed paper; microwave on 100% (high) 20 minutes, stirring after 10 minutes. Cook until carrots are tender. Set aside.

Dissolve masa harina in 1 cup water; stir into soup. Cover with waxed paper; microwave on 70% (medium-high) 10 minutes, stirring after 5 minutes. Let stand 5 minutes before serving. Garnish with lime slice and dollop of yogurt.

Each serving contains:

Cal	Prot	Carb	Fib	Tot. Fat	Sat. Fat	Chol	Sodium
196	15g	19g	4g	7g	1g	30mg	637mg

Azteca in a recipe title means masa harina or corn flour is used in the dish.

Pescado al Jardín

Garden-style Fish

Pimiento-stuffed olives combine with seasonings to create a delectable flavor.

Power level: high, medium-high
Cooking time: 13 minutes
Servings: 4 to 5

1/4 cup chopped onion

1/4 cup chopped bell pepper

1 garlic clove, chopped

1 tablespoon olive oil

1/4 cup chopped pimiento-stuffed green olives

1/4 cup diced green chiles

1/2 teaspoon cilantro seeds, crushed

1 teaspoon dried-leaf oregano, crushed

1 tablespoon lemon juice or lime juice

1-1/2 lbs. fish fillets

1/2 teaspoon paprika

2 tablespoons chopped fresh parsley or cilantro

Combine onion, bell pepper, garlic and olive oil in a 12" x 8" flat-bottom casserole. Cover with waxed paper; microwave on 100% (high) 2 minutes. Add olives, chiles, cilantro, oregano and lemon or lime juice; stir to combine. Cover with waxed paper; microwave on 70% (medium-high) 3 minutes. Push cooked vegetables to side of dish.

Arrange fish fillets in casserole; sprinkle with paprika. Spoon simmered vegetables over fish. Sprinkle with parsley or cilantro. Cover with waxed paper; microwave on 70% (medium-high) 8 minutes, turning dish after 4 minutes. Let stand 5 minutes. Fish at center of dish should flake easily with a fork. If more cooking is needed, cover and microwave on 70% (medium-high) 1 minute or until fish is done. Serve hot.

Each serving contains:

Cal	Prot	Carb	Fib	Tot. Fat	Sat. Fat	Chol	Sodium
165	26g	3g	1g	5g	1g	65mg	248mg

Pescado en Jugo de Naranja

Fish in Orange Juice

Orange juice combined with parsley creates a unique flavor.

Power level: high, medium-high
Cooking time: 11-1/2 minutes
Servings: 6

1 garlic clove, mashed

1/4 cup margarine

1/2 cup all-purpose flour

1/2 teaspoon paprika

1/2 teaspoon salt

1/2 teaspoon pepper

1-1/2 lbs. white-fish fillets

1/4 cup orange juice

3 tablespoons chopped fresh parsley

1 orange, sliced, if desired

Put garlic and margarine in a 12" x 8" flat-bottom casserole. Cover with waxed paper; microwave on 100% (high) 2 minutes.

In a shallow dish, combine flour, paprika, salt and pepper; coat fish fillets with flour mixture. Place each fillet in the casserole, coating both sides with garlic and melted margarine. Cover; microwave on 100% (high) 1-1/2 minutes, turn fillets over after 45 seconds.

Pour orange juice over fish; sprinkle with parsley. Cover with waxed paper; microwave on 70% (medium-high) 8 minutes, turning dish after 4 minutes. Let stand 5 minutes. Fish should flake easily. If more cooking is needed, cover and microwave on 70% (medium-high) 1 minute or longer. Garnish with orange slices, if desired. Serve hot.

Each serving contains:

Cal	Prot	Carb	Fib	Tot. Fat	Sat. Fat	Chol	Sodium
199	23g	10g	1g	7g	2g	54mg	364mg

Pescado Empanizado

Breaded Fish

Fish is always quick to prepare in the microwave and is tender and flaky.

Power level: high
Cooking time: 6 minutes
Servings: 4

1 tablespoon vegetable oil

1 cup fine dry bread crumbs

1 teaspoon paprika

1/4 teaspoon dried-leaf oregano, crushed

1/2 teaspoon salt

1/2 teaspoon azafrán or saffron, if desired

1/3 cup skim milk

1 lb. fish fillets

Spread oil in a 12" x 8" flat-bottom casserole. Combine bread crumbs, paprika, oregano, salt, and azafrán or saffron, if desired. Pour milk in a shallow dish. Dip each fillet in milk; then in crumb mixture. Place fillets in casserole. Cover with waxed paper; microwave on 100% (high) 2 minutes. Turn fillets over. Cover with waxed paper; microwave on 100% (high) 4 minutes, turning dish after 2 minutes. Let stand 5 minutes. Fish at center of dish should flake easily with a fork. If more cooking time is needed, cover and microwave on 100% (high) 1 minute or until done. Serve hot.

Each serving contains:

Cal	Prot	Carb	Fib	Tot. Fat	Sat. Fat	Chol	Sodium
240	25g	20g	1g	6g	1g	56mg	553mg

Photo front cover

Pescado en Escabeche

Fish Marinated in Vinegar

If you're missing ingredients, top cooked fillets with salsa.

Lower level: high
Cooking time: 5 minutes
Servings: 6

3 tablespoons olive oil

1-1/2 lbs. white-fish fillets, about 1/4-inch thick

Marinade:
1/2 cup chopped onion

2 garlic cloves, mashed

1/2 cup chopped bell pepper

1/4 cup diced green chile

1/2 teaspoon black pepper

1/2 cup white vinegar

1/2 teaspoon paprika

2 tablespoons lemon or lime juice

1/2 teaspoon dried-leaf oregano

1/4 teaspoon cilantro seeds, crushed

1/4 cup fresh parsley or cilantro

1/4 cup water

Pour oil into a 12" x 8" casserole. Place fish fillets in casserole, turning pieces to coat both sides with oil. Cover with waxed paper; microwave on 100% (high) 5 minutes, turning fish over after 2-1/2 minutes. Set fish aside.

Combine marinade ingredients in a bowl. Pour marinade over fish. Cover and refrigerate 12 to 24 hours. Chilled fish is ready to serve. Serve on lettuce or other greens.

Each serving contains:

Cal	Prot	Carb	Fib	Tot. Fat	Sat. Fat	Chol	Sodium
180	22g	5g	1g	8g	1g	54mg	94mg

❦ **Variation**
Add 1-1/2 cups chopped tomatoes and 1/2 cup tomato sauce to marinade. As an appetizer, cut fish in chunks. Serve in cocktail glasses with diced avocado and lime juice. Season to taste.

Pescado en Salsa Roja

Fish in Red Sauce

Salsa Roja is a thick red sauce that gives seafood a mild spicy taste.

Power level: high, medium-high
Cooking time: 16 minutes
Servings: 5 to 6

2 tablespoons vegetable oil

1-1/2 lbs. rock fish or red snapper fillets, or 1 lb. shrimp, cleaned

Salsa Roja:
1 tablespoon vegetable oil

1 (6-oz.) can tomato paste

1 cup water

1/4 cup chopped onion

3 garlic cloves, chopped

2 tablespoons red-chile powder

1/2 teaspoon dried-leaf oregano

1/2 teaspoon cumin

1 teaspoon salt

1 lime or lemon, cut in wedges

Pour oil into a 12" x 8" casserole. Place fish fillets or shrimp in dish, turning to coat both sides. Cover with waxed paper; microwave on 100% (high) 4 minutes, turning after 2 minutes. Set aside.

Place oil, tomato paste, water, onion, garlic, chile powder, oregano, cumin and salt in a blender or food processor. Process until puréed. Pour mixture into a 1-quart bowl. Cover with waxed paper; microwave on 70% (medium-high) 10 minutes, stirring every 3 minutes.

Pour cooked salsa over cooked fish. Cover with waxed paper; microwave on 70% (medium-high) 2 minutes. Fish is cooked if it flakes easily. Serve immediately with lime or lemon wedges.

Each serving contains:

Cal	Prot	Carb	Fib	Tot. Fat	Sat. Fat	Chol	Sodium
214	25g	9g	2g	9g	1g	42mg	472mg

Pescado en Salsa de Tomate con Arroz

Fish in Spicy Tomato Sauce with Rice

Fish is high in protein without added fat. It's truly simple to prepare in the microwave oven.

Power level: high
Cooking time: 7 to 8 minutes
Servings: 4

1/3 cup chopped onion

1 garlic clove, chopped

1 tablespoon lime juice

1/4 cup chopped green chile

2 tablespoons cilantro

1 (8-oz.) can tomato sauce

1 lb. fish fillets

Hot cooked rice

Cilantro for garnish, if desired

Put onion, garlic, lime juice, green chile and cilantro in a 1-1/2 quart casserole dish, cover with waxed paper and microwave on 100% (high) 2 minutes.

Purée vegetables and tomato sauce in blender. Set aside.

Lightly oil or spray with vegetable cooking spray the bottom of a 2-quart flat bottom casserole. Lay fish in casserole. Pour tomato mixture over fish. Cover with waxed paper; microwave on 100% (high) 5 to 6 minutes. Fish is cooked if it flakes easily. Serve on a bed of rice and garnish with cilantro, if desired.

Each serving contains:

Cal	Prot	Carb	Fib	Tot. Fat	Sat. Fat	Chol	Sodium
131	23g	7g	1g	1g	0	54mg	436mg

Antojitos de Pescado

Fish Rolls

If you like garlic and cilantro, you will enjoy these fish rolls. They are great as appetizers.

Power level: high
Cooking time: 4 to 6 minutes
Servings: 4

2 tablespoons chopped cilantro

1 teaspoon lime juice

2 garlic cloves, mashed

1/2 teaspoon red-chile powder

1 teaspoon vegetable oil

1 lb. fish fillets

1 lime, cut into quarters

Combine fresh cilantro leaves, lime juice, garlic, chile powder and vegetable oil in a 1-1/2 quart casserole dish. Set aside.

Cut fish fillets lengthwise into 1/2-inch strips. Combine fish fillets with cilantro mixture in casserole dish. Grease or spray with vegetable cooking spray a 12" x 8" flat-bottom casserole dish. Roll each fish-fillet strip in a roll, secure with a tooth pick if desired and place in casserole.

Cover with waxed paper and microwave on 100% (high) 4 to 6 minutes or until fish is done. Fish is done when it can be easily pierced with a fork. Squeeze lime juice over fish and serve.

Each serving contains:

Cal	Prot	Carb	Fib	Tot. Fat	Sat. Fat	Chol	Sodium
122	22g	3g	0	3g	0	54mg	96mg

Mariscos en Chile Rojo

Scallops in Red Chile

Red-chile sauce poured over scallops and vegetables makes this high-protein, lowfat fish an excellent choice for a meal.

Power level: high
Cooking time: 8 minutes
Servings: 4

1 lb. scallops, cut in half if scallops are large

1 tablespoon vegetable oil

2 garlic cloves, minced

1/2 teaspoon dried-leaf oregano, crushed

1/3 cup chopped onions

2 teaspoons red-chile powder

1/4 teaspoon salt

1 cup scallop liquid, reserved

2 tablespoons cornstarch

3 tablespoons chopped fresh cilantro or parsley

Cooked rice, if desired

Wash scallops, drain on paper towels and set aside. Combine vegetable oil, garlic, oregano, onions, red chile powder and salt in a 1-1/2-quart casserole dish. Cover with waxed paper. Microwave on 100% (high) 2 minutes, stirring after 1 minute. Add scallops and combine. Cover with waxed paper and microwave on 100% (high) 3 minutes, stirring after 1-1/2 minutes.

Drain scallops and vegetables, reserving scallop liquid. Set scallops and vegetables aside.

To the reserved scallop liquid add enough water to make 1 cup. Dissolve cornstarch in liquid. Pour over scallops. Top with cilantro or parsley. Cover with waxed paper and microwave on 100% (high) 3 minutes, stirring after 1-1/2 minutes. Serve over a bed of rice.

Each serving contains:

Cal	Prot	Carb	Fib	Tot. Fat	Sat. Fat	Chol	Sodium
152	20g	8g	1g	5g	0	37mg	329mg

Caldillo de Pescado

Fish Soup

Enjoy your favorite seafood in this delicious soup.

Power level: high
Cooking time: 33 minutes
Servings: 6

2 tablespoons olive oil

1/4 cup chopped onion

2 garlic cloves, chopped

2 medium tomatoes, chopped

1/2 cup finely chopped celery

1 teaspoon azafrán or saffron

1 teaspoon dried-leaf oregano

1/2 teaspoon cilantro seeds, crushed

1 tablespoon red-chile powder

1/2 teaspoon salt

2 (8-oz.) bottles clam juice

3 cups water

1 lb. white fish, 1/2 lb. scallops and 1/2 lb. clams

1/4 cup fresh cilantro or parsley

1 lime, quartered

Combine oil, onion and garlic in a 5-quart casserole. Cover with a lid; microwave on 100% (high) 3 minutes. Add tomatoes, celery, azafrán or saffron, oregano, cilantro seeds, chile powder, salt, clam juice and water. Cover with a lid; microwave on 100% (high) 15 minutes. Add fish and shellfish. Cover and microwave on 100% (high) 15 minutes or until clams and/or mussels open.

To serve, fill individual bowls with Caldillo. Garnish with fresh cilantro or parsley and a squeeze of lime.

Each serving contains:

Cal	Prot	Carb	Fib	Tot. Fat	Sat Fat	Chol	Sodium
194	27g	7g	1g	7g	1g	64mg	509mg

❦   ❦   ❦

When traveling in Mexico, my husband makes a special trip to a seafood restaurant in Guaymas, Sonora to have this soup. It is similar to bouillabaisse.

Camarones con Verduras

Shrimp with Vegetables

A wonderful combination to serve over rice.

Power level: high
Cooking time: 9 minutes
Servings: 4 to 5

2 tablespoons olive oil

1/2 cup chopped onion

2 garlic cloves, chopped

1 medium tomato, chopped

1/2 cup chopped bell pepper

1/4 cup chopped green chiles

1 teaspoon paprika

1/4 teaspoon dried-leaf oregano

1/2 teaspoon salt

1 tablespoon lime or lemon juice

1 lb. medium shrimp, peeled and veined

1 lime, quartered

Place all ingredients except shrimp and lime into a 2-quart casserole. Cover with waxed paper; microwave on 100% (high) 4 minutes, stirring after 2 minutes. Stir in shrimp. Cover with waxed paper; microwave on 100% (high) 5 minutes, stirring after 2-1/2 minutes. Shrimp is done when it turns opaque. Squeeze lime over shrimp dish. Serve immediately.

Each serving contains:

Cal	Prot	Carb	Fib	Tot. Fat	Sat. Fat	Chol	Sodium
169	19g	7g	1g	7g	1g	138mg	351mg

Comidas de Verduras

Vegetable dishes in traditional Mexican cuisine are usually served with a cheese sauce. Vegetables are also added to meat dishes or simmered and used as a topping for meats, poultry or fish dishes.

White cheese, a Mexican tradition, was commonly made from *leche cuajada* or curdled milk. A pouch was made of *manta*, muslin or several layers of cheesecloth. Curdled milk was poured into the pouch and hung in the coolest part of the house. They dripped into a bucket for 3 to 4 days until a white mass of cheese formed in the pouch. Then, a sweet, white, pear-shape cheese was removed. It was used to make quesadillas, served with fruits or added to vegetables. Even today, you can buy white cheese and goat cheese in the old markets of Ciudad Juárez.

At our house, we almost always had cheese in our vegetable dishes, whether it was squash, corn or green beans. I particularly liked sliced summer squash with Monterey Jack or mild Cheddar cheese.

Baking was a common method of preparing vegetables and fruits, such as *Manzanas Asadas* (Baked Apples), and *Plátanos Dulces* (Candied Plantains). The plantain is a cousin to the banana. They are larger and firmer than bananas. In Mexico this starchy fruit, which is always cooked, is treated as a vegetable.

Berenjena y Chile con Queso

Eggplant & Chile Cheese

A winning combination.

Power level: high, medium-high
Cooking time: 19 to 21 minutes
Servings: 6

1/2 lb. ground turkey

**1 eggplant, cubed and peeled
(4 cups)**

1/2 cup water

1 egg or 2 egg whites

1/4 cup chopped onion

1/2 cup oatmeal

1/2 teaspoon cumin

**1/2 teaspoon dried-leaf oregano,
crushed**

1/4 teaspoon paprika

**1/2 cup shredded Cheddar
cheese (2 oz.)**

**1/2 cup chopped green chiles or
1 (4-oz.) can diced green chiles**

Place turkey in a 1-1/2-quart casserole. Cover with waxed paper and microwave on 100% (high) 2 minutes, stirring after 1 minute. Drain liquid from turkey; set aside.

Place eggplant and water in a 1-1/2-quart casserole. Cover with waxed paper; microwave on 100% (high) 9 minutes, rotating after 4-1/2 minutes. Let stand 5 minutes. Drain liquid; mash eggplant. In a bowl, combine eggplant, turkey and remaining ingredients; blend well. Set aside. Grease or spray with vegetable cooking spray a microwave-safe ring mold or a round, 1-1/2-quart casserole. Place an inverted custard cup in center of casserole. Pour in eggplant mixture. Cover with waxed paper; microwave on 70% (medium-high) 8 minutes, rotating after 4 minutes. Let stand 5 minutes. If more cooking is needed, continue 2 minutes. Serve immediately.

Each serving contains:

Cal	Prot	Carb	Fib	Tot. Fat	Sat. Fat	Chol	Sodium
186	15g	10g	3g	10g	4g	72mg	104mg

Chayote al Horno

Baked Chayotes

Try a vegetarian burrito. Roll this squash mixture in a tortilla.

Power level: high, medium-high
Cooking time: 12 minutes
Servings: 4

2 chayote or zucchini squash, peeled and cut into chunks (about 2 to 2-1/2 cups)

1/4 cup water

1/2 cup chopped tomatoes (about 1 medium-size tomato)

1/4 cup chopped roasted green chiles, page 3, or 1 (4-oz.) can diced green chiles

1 garlic clove, chopped

1/4 teaspoon dried-leaf oregano

Salt to taste

1/4 cup shredded Cheddar cheese (1 oz.)

Put chunked chayote or zucchini squash in a 1-1/2-quart casserole dish. Add water, cover with waxed paper and microwave on 100% (high) 5 to 6 minutes, stirring after 3 minutes. Zucchini may take 1 to 2 minutes less time to cook. Cook until squash is tender when pierced with fork. Drain liquid and set aside.

Put tomatoes, chiles, garlic, oregano and salt in a 1-1/2-quart casserole dish. Cover with waxed paper and microwave on 100% (high) 2 minutes. Add chayote or zucchini squash to vegetables and mix together. Cover with waxed paper and microwave on 70% (medium-high) 4 minutes, stirring after 2 minutes. Top with shredded cheese and microwave on 100% (high) 30 seconds until cheese melts.

Each serving contains:

Cal	Prot	Carb	Fib	Tot. Fat	Sat. Fat	Chol	Sodium
54	3g	6g	1g	3g	2g	7mg	49mg

Chayotes Rellenos

Stuffed Chayote

Serve this side dish at your next Mexican buffet.

Power level: high
Cooking time: 17 minutes
Servings: 4

1/2 lb. ground turkey or ground beef

2 chayote or zucchini squash

2 tablespoons water

3 tablespoons chopped onion

1/4 cup chopped green chile or 1 (4-oz.) can diced green chiles

1/3 cup chopped tomatoes

1 garlic clove, chopped

1/2 teaspoon cumin

1/4 teaspoon dried-leaf oregano, crushed

1 teaspoon vegetable oil or meat broth

1/4 cup shredded Cheddar cheese (1 oz.)

Place ground turkey or beef in a 1-1/2-quart casserole dish. Cover with waxed paper and microwave on 100% (high) 4 minutes, stirring after 2 minutes. Drain meat; set aside.

Cut chayote or zucchini in half lengthwise. Remove chayote seed. Place in a pie plate with cut surface down. Add 2 tablespoons water. Cover with waxed paper and microwave on 100% (high) 5 to 6 minutes, rearranging the squash after 3 minutes. Zucchini takes about 1 to 2 minutes less time to cook. Let stand 5 minutes. Drain liquid. Scoop out pulp, leaving a shell. Chop squash pulp and add to meat. Set aside.

Combine remaining ingredients except cheese in a small bowl; cover with waxed paper. Microwave on 100% (high) 3 minutes, stirring after 1-1/2 minutes. Combine all mixtures.

Fill squash shells with mixture. Cover with waxed paper. Microwave on 100% (high) 4 minutes. Top with cheese and microwave on 100% (high) 30 seconds or until cheese melts. Serve.

Each serving contains:

Cal	Prot	Carb	Fib	Tot. Fat	Sat. Fat	Chol	Sodium
196	17g	6g	1g	12g	4g	47mg	96mg

❦ Variation

Add 1/2 cup cooked corn to the meat mixture.

A *chayote* (also referred to as a vegetable pear) is a pale green, pear-shaped summer squash. The skin is deeply ribbed in a lengthwise direction. The tough skin must be peeled before cooking unless using it for Chayotes Rellenos (Stuffed Chayote). They can be used in recipes calling for zucchini squash or eaten raw in salads or relish dishes. The taste is a little like a cucumber. If chayote squash is not available, use zucchini squash.

Calabaza con Queso

Squash with Cheese

If you grow squash in your garden, here's a wonderful dish that is easy to prepare and tastes great!

Power level: high
Cooking time: 15 minutes
Servings: 6

2 tablespoons margarine

1/4 cup chopped onion

1 garlic clove, chopped

1/4 cup chopped bell pepper

3 cups thinly sliced summer squash, such as zucchini, cocozelle or straight or crookneck squash

1/4 teaspoon salt, if desired

1/2 cup water

1/2 cup shredded Monterey Jack or jalapeño cheese (2 oz.)

Combine margarine, onion, garlic and bell pepper in a 2-quart casserole. Cover with waxed paper; microwave on 100% (high) 3 minutes. Stir in squash, salt, if desired, and water. Cover with waxed paper; microwave on 100% (high) 10 minutes, stirring after 5 minutes. Squash should be tender. If more cooking is needed, cover with waxed paper; microwave on 100% (high) 1 minute or until tender.

Drain liquid from squash; stir in 1/4 cup cheese. Sprinkle remaining cheese over squash. Cover with waxed paper; microwave on 100% (high) 1 minute or until cheese melts. Serve hot.

Each serving contains:

Cal	Prot	Carb	Fib	Tot. Fat	Sat. Fat	Chol	Sodium
78	3g	4g	1g	6g	3g	8mg	99mg

In the early 1920s the Amador Hotel in Las Cruces, New Mexico was the showplace of the Southwest with its plush European decor and little theater. Many famous people from the Eastern United States stayed there on their way to Mexico or the West Coast. The magician Houdini, General John Pershing, John Dean of New York opera fame and a number of Hollywood celebrities were among the guests.

The Amador Hotel had a varied cuisine, from Mexican to Continental. My great-aunt Lupe, who was their cook for several years, often told me that their most requested dish was her Calabaza con Queso. Calabaza—squash or pumpkin in any form—was very popular.

Lupe told of an hilarious occasion when the owner of the Amador Hotel brought her two packets of dehydrated carrots, thinking them to be pumpkin. She asked Lupe to make the guests a pumpkin pie. Lupe soaked the dehydrated carrots, sliced and spiced them until she got them to taste as close to pumpkin as possible. Well, the guests were so thrilled with the pie that several of them begged her to share her secret recipe with them!

Chile con Elote

Chile with Corn

Creamed corn gives this dish a creamy consistency when baked. It's a fine dish to accompany any Mexican entrée.

Power level: high, medium-high
Cooking time: 17 to 18 minutes
Servings: 6

2 tablespoons margarine

1/4 cup chopped onion

1/4 cup chopped bell pepper

2 tablespoons all-purpose flour

1/2 teaspoon salt

1/2 teaspoon paprika

1/2 cup chopped green chiles

1 egg

1 (8-oz.) can cream-style corn

1 (16-oz.) can whole-kernel corn, drained

1/2 cup shredded Cheddar cheese (2 oz.)

Combine margarine, onion and bell pepper in a 1-1/2-quart casserole. Cover with waxed paper; microwave on 100% (high) 2 minutes. Stir in flour, salt, paprika, chiles, egg and corn. Cover with waxed paper; microwave on 70% (medium-high) 14 to 15 minutes, stirring after 7 minutes. Top with cheese; microwave on 70% (medium-high) 1 minute. Let stand 5 minutes before serving.

Each serving contains:

Cal	Prot	Carb	Fib	Tot. Fat	Sat. Fat	Chol	Sodium
183	7g	25g	2g	8g	3g	45mg	577mg

Cacerola de Elote

Corn Casserole

A hearty meal in itself: Serve with fresh beans and warm flour tortillas.

Power level: high, medium-high
Cooking time: 16 to 17 minutes
Servings: 4

1 lb. ground beef

2 tablespoons margarine

1 (8-3/4-oz.) can whole-kernel corn, drained

1/4 cup yellow cornmeal

1/2 teaspoon salt

1/4 teaspoon ground oregano

1/2 teaspoon onion powder

1/4 cup dairy sour cream

1/2 cup all-purpose flour

1/2 teaspoon baking powder

1/4 cup chopped green chiles

1/2 cup shredded Cheddar cheese (2 oz.)

Crumble ground beef into a 1-1/2-quart casserole or microwave browning dish. Cover with waxed paper; microwave on 100% (high) 4 to 5 minutes, stirring after 2 minutes. Drain fat; set aside.

Place margarine in a glass bowl; microwave on 100% (high) 45 seconds. Stir in corn, cornmeal, salt, oregano, onion powder and sour cream. Purée mixture in a blender. Stir flour and baking powder into mixture. Stir in beef and chiles.

Grease or spray with vegetable cooking spray a microwave-safe ring mold. Or place an inverted custard cup in center of a round casserole. Add batter. Cover with waxed paper; microwave on 70% (medium-high) 10 minutes, turning dish after 5 minutes. Top with cheese. Cover with waxed paper; microwave on 70% (medium-high) 1 minute. Let stand 5 minutes. Serve hot.

Each serving contains:

Cal	Prot	Carb	Fib	Tot. Fat	Sat. Fat	Chol	Sodium
576	36g	32g	2g	34g	14g	120mg	705mg

Ensalada de Espinaca

Spinach Salad

A great salad to serve at any meal.

Power level: high
Cooking time: 5 minutes
Servings: 4

1 bunch spinach leaves

2 tablespoons olive oil

1 small onion, sliced thin

3 garlic cloves, minced

2 tablespoons red-wine vinegar

3 tablespoons water

1/4 cup sliced olives

2 medium tomatoes, sliced or quartered

1/2 teaspoon crushed red-chile pepper

1/4 cup red bell pepper, cut into strips, if desired

1/2 cup shredded Cheddar cheese (2 oz.)

Wash spinach leaves and remove stems. Remove as much moisture as possible by draining leaves on paper towels. Place leaves in a bowl and refrigerate until ready to use.

Combine oil, onion and garlic in a 1-1/2 quart dish and microwave on 100% (high) 5 minutes, stirring onions after 2-1/2 minutes. Add vinegar, water, olives, tomatoes, chile pepper and red bell pepper if desired. Pour over spinach leaves and toss. Sprinkle with shredded cheese. Chill before serving.

Each serving contains:

Cal	Prot	Carb	Fib	Tot. Fat	Sat Fat	Chol	Sodium
153	5g	8g	2g	12g	4g	15mg	132mg

Ensalada Mexicana

Taco Salad

"Meal-in-a-salad."

Power level: high, medium-high
Cooking time: 10 minutes
Servings: 6

1 lb. ground beef or turkey

3 tablespoons Taco Seasoning Mix, page 8, or 1 (1-1/4-oz.) pkg. taco seasoning mix

1 (15-oz.) can pinto beans

1 small head lettuce

2 tomatoes, chopped

1/2 cup chopped bell pepper

1/3 cup chopped onion

1/3 cup chopped celery

1/2 cup sliced ripe olives

1 cup shredded Cheddar cheese (4 oz.)

6 cups Tortilla Chips, page 44, or 1 (11-oz.) bag tortilla chips, plain or flavored

1 cup Taco Sauce, page 9, or PACE® Picante Sauce

Crumble ground beef or turkey into a 2-quart casserole. Cover with waxed paper; microwave on 100% (high) 5 minutes, stir after 2-1/2 minutes. Drain fat; stir in seasoning mix and beans. Cover with waxed paper; microwave meat mixture on 70% (medium-high) 5 minutes, stirring after 2-1/2 minutes.

Rinse lettuce; pat dry with towels. Tear lettuce into pieces; place in large bowl. Add tomatoes, bell pepper, onion, celery, 1/4 cup olives and 1/2 cup cheese; toss. Make a well in the middle. Spoon meat mixture into center of salad. Top with remaining olives and cheese.

Place tortilla chips around edge. Serve remaining chips in a separate bowl with Taco Sauce.

Each serving contains:

Cal	Prot	Carb	Fib	Tot. Fat	Sat. Fat	Chol	Sodium
768	37g	75g	18g	39g	11g	86mg	529mg

Plátanos Dulces

Candied Plantains

Plantains must be cooked before eating. They contain more starch and less sugar than bananas. Or, use firm, nearly ripe bananas.

Power level: high
Cooking time: 8 minutes
Servings: 4

2 plantains

3 tablespoons margarine

3 tablespoons piloncillo (panocha) or dark-brown sugar

3 tablespoons granulated sugar

Peel plantains; cut lengthwise into quarters. Cut each quarter into 3-inch pieces; set aside. Place margarine in a glass pie plate. Cover with waxed paper; microwave on 100% (high) 1 minute or until melted. Add plantain pieces. Cover with waxed paper; microwave on 100% (high) 6 minutes, turning pieces over after 3 minutes.

Sprinkle with brown sugar and granulated sugar. Microwave, uncovered, on 100% (high) 1 minute. Let stand 5 minutes. Plantain pieces should be soft when pierced with a fork. If more cooking is needed, cover and microwave on 100% (high) 1 minute or until tender. Serve warm.

Each serving contains:

Cal	Prot	Carb	Fib	Tot. Fat	Sat. Fat	Chol	Sodium
270	2g	55g	5g	7g	2g	0	115mg

If plantains are green, keep at room temperature until brown and starting to soften. Ripening may take several days.

Ejotes con Queso

Green Beans with Cheese

*Colorful and delicious
vegetable dish.*

Power level: high
Cooking time: 5 to 6 minutes
Servings: 4

1 tablespoon vegetable oil

1/4 cup chopped onion

1 garlic clove, chopped

**1/4 teaspoon dried-leaf oregano,
crushed**

**1 (16-oz.) can whole green
beans, drained**

1/4 teaspoon salt

1/4 cup chopped green chiles

**1 cup shredded Monterey Jack
cheese (4 oz.)**

1 tomato, cut into wedges

Combine oil, onion, garlic and
oregano in a 1-1/2-quart casserole.
Cover with waxed paper; microwave on 100% (high) 2 minutes. Stir
in green beans, salt, chiles and
1/2 cup cheese. Cover with waxed
paper; microwave on 100% (high)
3 minutes.

Arrange tomato wedges on top of
green beans; sprinkle with remaining cheese. Cover with waxed
paper; microwave on 100% (high)
45 seconds or until cheese melts.
Serve hot.

Each serving contains:

Cal	Prot	Carb	Fib	Tot. Fat	Sat. Fat	Chol	Sodium
173	9g	9g	2g	12g	6g	25mg	574mg

Barquitos de Oro

Little Golden Boats

Prepared this way, yams have the appearance of little yellow boats.

Power level: high
Cooking time: 7 to 8 minutes
Servings: 2

1 yam (about 3/4 lb.)

1/4 teaspoon ground cinnamon

1/4 cup whipping cream

1 tablespoon drained crushed pineapple

2 tablespoons roasted piñon nuts or chopped blanched almonds

1/2 cup whipped cream

Scrub yam; pierce with a fork to prevent rupture during baking. Place in a glass pie plate; microwave on 100% (high) 7 to 8 minutes, turning yam over after 3-1/2 minutes. Yam is cooked when it can be pierced easily with a fork. If more cooking is needed, microwave on 100% (high) 1 minute or until tender. Let yam cool.

Cut cooled, cooked yam in half, lengthwise. Scoop out flesh, placing it in a small bowl; reserve hollowed-out skins. Stir cinnamon and whipping cream into flesh. Whip until mixture is very light. Stir in pineapple and nuts. Spoon mixture back into yam-skin shells. Chill boats 15 minutes or until ready to serve. To serve, top with whipped cream.

Each serving contains:

Cal	Prot	Carb	Fib	Tot. Fat	Sat. Fat	Chol	Sodium
216	2g	6g	0	21g	13g	74mg	23mg

❧   ❧   ❧

In my recipe Little Golden Boats, I use piñon nuts. There is a tradition of using piñon nuts harvested from the pine forests of the Southwest. My mother recalls her grandmother getting piñon nuts from an old man named Don Atenójenes. She would give the man a 50- to 100-pound sack of dried corn to take with him to the mountains of Northern New Mexico. The corn was to put out for the squirrels as food to compensate for our harvest of piñones. He would faithfully return with a 100-pound sack of piñones which would last for a year.

My mother's job was to separate chaff from nuts, which she would do on a very windy day. She would take a pail of piñones and pour them from a height of 3 to 4 feet, letting them fall into a large tub. The wind would in turn blow away any dried leaves, sticks, sand or other foreign material. Grandmother would then spread the piñones on a table where any other foreign particles would be removed by hand.

Piñones were then roasted in big, square roasting pans in the kitchen wood-stove oven under grandmother's watchful eye. She stirred the nuts with a long-handled spoon to keep them from burning. The aroma of roasting piñones was a lasting pleasant memory of my mother's.

After the roasting, grandmother would sell the nuts in quarter-pound sacks for a nickel, half-pound sacks for a dime, and pound sacks for a quarter. A paper sack of freshly roasted piñones was a must for football fans at hometown games.

While teaching in San Rafael in Northern New Mexico, I thought I could engage my family in collecting piñones. My students told me of a piñon grove and their practice of putting grain out for the squirrels to eat while they were gathering piñones. With a sheet, bucket and a bag of grain, we set out to harvest nuts. We learned that the piñon trees do not always bear a bumper crop. We returned empty-handed, but the squirrels ate well that autumn.

Cacerola de Papas con Chile

Potatoes with Chile Casserole

Chile and cheese accent potatoes.

Power level: medium-high
Cooking time: 14 minutes
Servings: 6 servings

4 or 5 medium-size potatoes (about 1-1/2 lbs.)

1/4 cup chopped green chiles, or 1 (4-oz.) can diced green chiles

2 tablespoons chopped onion

1/2 cup chicken broth or 1/2 teaspoon instant chicken bouillon granules in 1/2 cup warm water

1/2 cup shredded Cheddar cheese (2 oz.)

Peel and thinly slice potatoes, set aside. Combine chiles and onion, set aside. Lightly grease or spray with vegetable cooking spray bottom of an 8-inch-square casserole dish. Layer potatoes, chiles, onion, broth and cheese. Make 3 layers, ending with cheese.

Cover with waxed paper and microwave on 70% (medium-high) 14 minutes, turning dish after 7-1/2 minutes. Allow to set 5 minutes. Potatoes are done when pierced with a fork. If more cooking is needed, cook 3 to 5 minutes more or until done. Serve warm.

Each serving contains:

Cal	Prot	Carb	Fib	Tot. Fat	Sat. Fat	Chol	Sodium
168	6g	30g	3g	3g	2g	10mg	68mg

Camotes Dulces

Candied Yams

Cooking yams at a low setting allows the sugar mixture to crystallize.

Power level: high, medium-low,
    medium-high
Cooking time: 37 minutes
Servings: 6

1-1/2 lbs. yam

1/2 cup water

1/3 cup piloncillo (panocha) or lightly packed dark-brown sugar

1/3 cup granulated sugar

In cooking, sweet potatoes and yams are generally considered interchangeable. Yet they are two different vegetables. Yams are sweeter and more moist than sweet potatoes.

Scrub yams; cut into 1/2-inch slices. Place yam slices and water in 2-1/2-quart casserole. Cover with waxed paper; microwave on 100% (high) 12 minutes, rearrange slices after 6 minutes. Yam slices should be tender when pierced with fork. Cool slices 15 minutes. Peel skins; set slices aside.

Oil or spray with vegetable cooking spray a 12" x 8" flat-bottom casserole. Combine sugars in a small bowl. Dip each slice into sugar mixture to coat both sides; arrange slices in rows in casserole. Microwave, uncovered, on 30% (medium-low) 15 minutes. Rotate dish; microwave on 70% (medium-high) 10 minutes. Let stand 5 minutes. Serve hot or cold.

Each serving contains:

Cal	Prot	Carb	Fib	Tot. Fat	Sat. Fat	Chol	Sodium
205	2g	50g	3g	0	0	0	18mg

Gazpacho

*Great served chilled on a hot day
or serve hot on a cold day.*

Power level: high
Cooking time: 6 minutes
Servings: 5 cups

1 (7-1/2-oz.) can whole tomatoes

3 cups tomato juice

1/4 cup chopped green onions

1/2 cup chopped celery

1/2 cup chopped cucumbers

**1 jalapeño pepper, finely
chopped**

1 garlic clove, finely chopped

1 tablespoon lime juice

**2 tablespoons apple cider
vinegar**

❦ **Variation**
Add diced avocados or cooked,
shelled shrimp.

Chop tomatoes and put into a 2-
quart bowl, add remaining ingredients. Mix well. Refrigerate 1 hour
before serving.

To serve hot, after refrigerating
Gazpacho 1 hour, place in a 2-quart
bowl or measuring cup, cover with
waxed paper and microwave on
100% (high) 6 minutes, stirring after
3 minutes.

Each serving contains:

Cal	Prot	Carb	Fib	Tot. Fat	Sat. Fat	Chol	Sodium
44	2g	11g	2g	0	0	0	610mg

Caldillo de Maíz Azul

Blue Corn Stew

Surprise your guests with this unusual dish. Blue-corn batter cooks into the form of a dumpling.

Power level: high
Cooking time: 24 minutes
Servings: 6

4 cups beef broth or 4 teaspoons instant beef bouillon granules dissolved in 4 cups hot water

1 (8-oz.) can whole tomatoes, chopped

1/4 cup chopped onion

1/4 cup chopped green chiles or 1 (4-oz.) can diced green chiles

1/4 teaspoon whole cominos, crushed

1/4 teaspoon dried-leaf oregano

3/4 cup plus 1 tablespoon blue cornmeal

1-1/2 teaspoon baking powder

1/4 teaspoon salt

1 tablespoon vegetable oil

1/2 cup skim milk

Combine beef broth, tomatoes, onion, chiles, cominos and oregano in a 3-quart bowl. Cover with waxed paper and microwave on 100% (high) 12 to 14 minutes, stirring after 6 minutes or until broth begins to boil.

Gently mix together blue-corn meal, baking powder, salt, vegetable oil and milk; do not overstir.

Drop blue-corn batter on top of boiling broth by teaspoonfuls (makes about 12 teaspoonfuls). Microwave, uncovered, on 100% (high) 12 minutes, stirring after 6 minutes. Cut blue-corn dumpling in half to test for doneness. If dumplings are not done, cook another 1 to 2 minutes. Pour into bowls and serve.

Each serving contains:

Cal	Prot	Carb	Fib	Tot. Fat	Sat. Fat	Chol	Sodium
120	5g	19g	2g	3g	0	1mg	244mg

Ã Variation
Add 1 cup shredded, cooked beef or chicken with broth and vegetables.

Postres y Bebidas

A shopping trip to Ciudad Juárez was one of my childhood delights. I particularly liked going to the candy vendors in the mercado. I remember standing on my tiptoes and surveying all the different colorful candies. There would be *dulce de coco* or coconut candy, various types of *jamoncillos* or fudge candies and *penuche,* a brown-sugar fudge among others. My search would usually continue until I spotted my favorite, an anise-flavored caramel stick called *melcocha.* One stick of melcocha would last the whole trip home.

No neighborhood was complete without a *panadería* or bakery. The aroma of the sweet breads would attract the attention of the neighborhood. I remember the piles of *pan dulce* in the bakery display case. Pan dulce came in an array of shapes and colors. There were *cuernitos* or crescent-shaped sweet rolls, *empanadas* or turnovers, *polvorones* or shortbread cookies, *rosquitas* or doughnut-shaped cookies and *pan de huevo* or egg sweet rolls. Each had its own colored sweetened-egg frosting: pinks, yellows and whites.

After our purchase from the *panadería*, we would go home to have *pan dulce* with Mexican Cocoa or a glass of *horchata*, a delicious rice drink.

Flan

Caramel Custard

Flan is served as a molded custard, topped with a caramel sauce. Be careful not to overcook the sugar mixture because the caramel will crystallize before it can coat the custard cups.

Power level: high, medium
Cooking time: 27 to 28 minutes
Servings: 4

1/2 cup sugar

1/3 cup water

1/3 cup nonfat dry milk powder

1-1/2 cups lowfat milk

1 egg plus 2 egg whites

1/4 cup sugar

1 teaspoon vanilla extract

1 tablespoon cornstarch

For caramel coating combine 1/2 cup sugar and 1/3 cup water in a glass bowl. Microwave on 100% (high) 6 to 7 minutes, stirring after 3 minutes. Caramel mixture is ready when it is golden in color. Pour equal amounts of caramel mixture into each of 4 custard cups. Rotate cups coating side and bottoms; set aside. Add milk powder to lowfat milk and stir. Heat milk in a separate glass bowl on 100% (high) 2 minutes. Beat together eggs, 1/4 cup sugar, vanilla and cornstarch in a small glass bowl. Slowly blend egg mixture into heated milk. Set aside.

Pour about 1-1/2 cups water into 8-inch-square flat-bottom casserole; microwave on 100% (high) 4 minutes or until water boils. Leave casserole with hot water in microwave. Pour egg mixture into coated custard cups. Set each cup in hot water in microwave. Microwave on 50% (medium) 15 minutes. Remove from microwave; let stand 5 minutes in hot water. Insert knife into flan; if it comes out clean, flan is done. Refrigerate until cool.

To unmold cooled flan, invert each cup onto a dessert plate. Lift custard cup from flan. If flan does not dislodge when cup is lifted, run a sharp knife between flan and side of custard cup; then invert. Refrigerate flan until ready to serve.

Each serving contains:

Cal	Prot	Carb	Fib	Tot. Fat	Sat. Fat	Chol	Sodium
235	8g	46g	0	2g	1g	58mg	121mg

❦ Variation

For a lighter flan, omit caramel coating altogether and prepare flan as directed. After preparation, unmold flan and pour Fruit Sauce, page 133, over flan.

❦ ❦ ❦

Flan is a recipe that dates back to the period of the Spanish Conquistadors. Its popularity continues to grow. You can use other flavorings or add grated coconut to the mixture before cooking. As an added garnish, top each serving with a tablespoon of meringue or whipped cream. Sprinkle with pecans.

Arroz con Leche

Rice Pudding

Serve this creamy rice pudding hot or cold.

Power level: high
Cooking time: 12 minutes
Servings: 4 (1/2-cup) servings

1 cup uncooked quick-cooking rice

1 cup water

2 egg whites

3/4 cup lowfat milk

3 tablespoons sugar

1/2 teaspoon vanilla extract

1/4 cup raisins, if desired

Ground cinnamon

Combine rice and water in a deep 3-quart casserole. Cover with a lid; microwave on 100% (high) 8 minutes or until water is absorbed and rice is tender. Let stand 5 minutes.

Beat together egg whites, milk, sugar and vanilla in a small bowl. Add egg mixture and raisins, if desired, to cooked rice; stir well to blend. Cover with waxed paper; microwave on 100% (high) 4 minutes, stirring after 2 minutes. Pour rice pudding into 4 dessert dishes; sprinkle with cinnamon. Serve warm or chilled.

Each serving contains:

Cal	Prot	Carb	Fib	Tot. Fat	Sat. Fat	Chol	Sodium
235	6g	49g	1g	1g	0	2mg	53mg

Capirotada

Bread Pudding

Bread pudding is a family favorite.

Power level: high
Cooking time: 7 minutes
Servings: 6

3 tablespoons piloncillo (panocha) or dark-brown sugar

1 cup apple juice

1/3 cup raisins

1 egg or 2 egg whites

1/2 teaspoon vanilla extract

1 tablespoon powdered sugar

4 slices whole-wheat or white bread, cut into cubes

3 tablespoons pecan pieces

2/3 cup shredded mild Cheddar cheese (2-2/3 oz.)

❦ ❦ ❦

Capirotada was a standard for the holidays. My mother would prepare it in a large pan, making enough for family and friends who stopped by to wish us Feliz Navidad, a Merry Christmas. My recipe is an adaptation of my mother's recipe.

Combine brown sugar, apple juice and raisins in a glass bowl; microwave on 100% (high) 3 minutes. Allow to cool.

Beat together egg or egg whites, vanilla and powdered sugar in a small bowl. Add egg mixture to raisin mixture, stirring to blend; set mixture aside.

Grease or spray with vegetable cooking spray a 1-1/2-quart casserole; alternately layer bread cubes, raisin mixture, pecans and cheese. Repeat layers. Make cheese final layer. Cover with waxed paper; microwave on 100% (high) 4 minutes, rotating dish after 2 minutes. Let stand 5 minutes. Serve hot or cold.

Each serving contains:

Cal	Prot	Carb	Fib	Tot. Fat	Sat. Fat	Chol	Sodium
218	7g	30g	2g	9g	3g	49mg	241mg

Natillas

Custard

*A smooth custard, especially good
served with fresh pineapple.*

Power level: high
Cooking time: 7 minutes
Servings: 8 (1-/2 cup) servings

2 cups lowfat milk

1/2 cup sugar

**3 eggs, separated, or 1 egg,
  separated, plus 2 egg whites**

3 tablespoons cornstarch

**2 tablespoons nonfat dry milk
  powder**

1-1/2 teaspoons vanilla extract

1/4 teaspoon cream of tartar

1 tablespoon sugar

**Ground cinnamon or ground
  nutmeg**

Combine milk, sugar, egg yolks,
cornstarch and dry milk in a 2-quart
casserole; beat until blended. Cover
with waxed paper; microwave on
100% (high) 7 minutes or until thick-
ened, stirring every 2 minutes. Stir in
vanilla; set aside.

Beat egg whites in a small bowl,
gradually adding cream of tartar and
1 tablespoon sugar, until egg whites
are stiff. Fold beaten egg whites into
pudding mixture. Pour into 8 individual serving dishes. Refrigerate until
cooled and set. To serve, sprinkle
with cinnamon or nutmeg.

Each serving contains:

Cal	Prot	Carb	Fib	Tot. Fat	Sat. Fat	Chol	Sodium
119	5g	20g	0	3g	1g	83mg	60mg

❦ Variation

To make Natillas de Chocolate, add
1/3 cup powdered unsweetened
cocoa and 2 tablespoons vegetable
oil to lowfat milk.

Tortilla de Fruta

Fruit-filled Tortilla

*Delicious topped with plain or
vanilla yogurt or with dollops
of whipped cream, if desired.*

Power level: medium-high, high
Cooking time: 5 minutes
Servings: 4

Strawberry Sauce:
1/3 cup sliced strawberries,
fresh or frozen

1 teaspoon sugar

1/3 cup apple juice

2 teaspoons cornstarch

Orange or Lemon Sauce:
2 tablespoons frozen
orange-juice or lemonade
concentrate can be substituted
for strawberries

1 (9- or 10-inch) flour tortilla

1-1/2 cups mixed fresh or
frozen fruit

1/3 cup sauce, above

Place all sauce ingredients in blender and purée. Pour mixture into small bowl, cover with waxed paper and microwave on 70% (medium-high) 2 minutes until mixture thickens. Set aside. Makes 1/3 cup.

Rub both sides of one flour tortilla with water. Place tortilla between 2 pieces of waxed paper. Microwave on 100% (high) 20 to 25 seconds or until tortilla is soft. Lightly grease or spray with vegetable cooking spray the inside of a round bowl 8" in diameter and 3" deep. Mold flour tortilla in bowl and microwave on 100% (high) 2-1/2 to 3 minutes or until flour tortilla is crisp. Remove molded tortilla and place on a plate.

Add fresh fruit and pour hot fruit sauce over fruit. Allow to cool in the refrigerator about 10 minutes. Cut into 4 sections, if desired, and serve.

Each serving contains:

Cal	Prot	Carb	Fib	Tot. Fat	Sat. Fat	Chol	Sodium
155	2g	36g	2g	1g	0	0	58mg

Papaya y Banana en miel

Papaya and Bananas in Syrup

Piloncillo *is Mexican brown sugar in the shape of a cone. If not available, substitute dark-brown sugar.*

Power level: medium-high
Cooking time: 4 minutes
Servings: 2

1/4 cup piloncillo (panocha) or dark-brown sugar

2 tablespoons water

1 papaya, cut in half

1 medium-size ripe banana

Maraschino cherries for garnish, if desired

Place piloncillo or brown sugar and water in a bowl and microwave on 70% (medium-high) 4 minutes or until brown sugar is dissolved, stirring after 2 minutes. If using piloncillo, break up piloncillo after 2 minutes so it will dissolve easier.

Wash and cut papaya in half, remove seeds. Scoop out flesh from papaya leaving a shell. Cut scooped-out papaya into pieces, set aside. Peel banana and cut lengthwise; then cut into slices. Combine papaya and bananas; spoon into papaya shells. Pour syrup over mixture; chill before serving. Garnish with maraschino cherries, if desired.

Each serving contains:

Cal	Prot	Carb	Fib	Tot. Fat	Sat. Fat	Chol	Sodium
213	2g	55g	4g	0	0	0	17mg

Papaya is a pear-shaped fruit. A ripe papaya has a smooth orange-yellow skin and will be soft when pressure is applied with the fingertips.

Peras de Dulce

Sweet Pears

Makes a tasty accompaniment to the main course— or as a dessert.

Power level: medium-high
Cooking time: 4 minutes
Servings: 4

2 pears or 1 (16-oz.) can pear halves, drained

4 to 6 whole cloves

1/4 cup piloncillo (panocha) or dark-brown sugar

4 tablespoons water

1/4 teaspoon ground cinnamon

Cut pears in half, place cut side down in a 1-1/2-quart flat-bottom casserole dish. Set aside. Put 1 clove in each pear half. Combine brown sugar, 4 tablespoons water and cinnamon in a small bowl and stir well. Pour syrup mixture over pears. Cover with waxed paper and microwave on 70% (medium-high) 4 minutes. Refrigerate until ready to serve. Remove whole cloves before eating.

Each serving contains:

Cal	Prot	Carb	Fib	Tot. Fat	Sat. Fat	Chol	Sodium
101	0	26g	2g	0	0	0	7mg

Sorbete de Mango

Mango Sherbet

Enjoy a taste of the tropics.

Power level: high
Cooking time: 2-1/2 minutes
Servings: 6 (1/2-cup) servings

1-1/2 cups skim milk

2 tablespoons nonfat dry milk powder

1/4 cup sugar

2 mangoes (about 10 oz. each), peeled and chopped (makes 1-1/2 to 2 cups mango pulp)

Put milk, dry milk and sugar in a glass bowl and microwave on 100% (high) 2-1/2 minutes or until sugar dissolves. Stir and set aside. Refrigerate 15 minutes.

Combine cooled milk mixture and chopped mango pieces in blender and blend 30 to 45 seconds or until mixture is well blended.

Pour mixture into an 12" x 8" casserole and freeze until mixture is solid (about 2-1/2 to 3 hours).

Place frozen mango sherbet in a mixer bowl. Break up sherbet then beat until mixture is creamy and fluffy. Spoon into 6 dessert dishes. Sherbet can be refrozen and reblended if need be.

Each serving contains:

Cal	Prot	Carb	Fib	Tot. Fat	Sat. Fat	Chol	Sodium
104	3g	24g	2g	0	0	1mg	41mg

❦ Variation
To make Strawberry Sherbet, substitute 2 cups sliced fresh or frozen strawberries for mangoes.

A mango, an oblong, round tropical fruit, ranges from a yellow-green to a red-yellow skin and has a yellow-orange pulp. Mangoes are high in vitamins A and C and potassium.

Torta de Maíz Azul

Blue Corn Cake

Combines Southwest Indian and Mexican ingredients.

Power level: medium
Cooking time: 5 to 6 minutes
Servings: 12

1 cup blue cornmeal

1/2 cup all-purpose flour

1 tablespoon baking powder

1/2 teaspoon salt

1/4 cup piloncillo (panocha) or dark-brown sugar

3 tablespoons vegetable oil

2 eggs or 3 egg whites

3/4 cup unsweetened apple juice

1/2 cup raisins, if desired

1/3 cup Panocha Syrup, page 138, if desired

Combine blue cornmeal, flour, baking powder, salt, piloncillo or brown sugar, vegetable oil, eggs or egg whites, apple juice, raisins. Mix together.

Grease or spray with vegetable cooking spray a microwave-safe ring mold or a round, glass cake dish. If you use a cake dish, place a greased inverted custard cup in the center to create a mold. Pour batter into mold or cake dish. Drizzle Panocha Syrup over batter, if desired.

Microwave on 50% (medium) 5 to 6 minutes, turning dish after 2-1/2 minutes. Cake is done when a toothpick inserted in the center of the cake comes out clean. If more cooking time is needed, microwave on 50% (medium) an additional 2 to 3 minutes or until done. Let stand 5 minutes before serving.

Each serving contains:

Cal	Prot	Carb	Fib	Tot. Fat	Sat. Fat	Chol	Sodium
129	3g	20g	1g	5g	1g	36mg	184mg

Miel de Panocha

Panocha Syrup (Brown-sugar Syrup)

Many Mexican postres (desserts) are topped with brown-sugar syrup. Miel de Panocha is an excellent topping for sopaipillas.

Power level: high
Cooking time: 14 minutes
Servings: 1-1/3 cups

1 cup water

1/2 cup piloncillo (panocha) or dark-brown sugar

1/8 teaspoon vanilla

2 tablespoons pecans, if desired

❦ Variation
Add 2 tablespoons of roasted piñon nuts.

Combine water and panocha or dark brown sugar in a 2-quart bowl. Microwave uncovered on 100% (high) 14 to 16 minutes, stirring after 7 minutes, or until syrup starts to thicken. Be careful not to over-cook as the syrup will harden as it cools. Add vanilla and pecan pieces if desired.

Each tablespoon contains:

Cal	Prot	Carb	Fib	Tot. Fat	Sat. Fat	Chol	Sodium
20	0	5g	0	0	0	0	2mg

Cajeta

Caramel Candy

Literally translated, Cajeta means "in a box."

Power level: high
Cooking time: 26 minutes
Servings: 1-1/4 cups

1-3/4 cups lowfat milk

1 cup granulated sugar

1/2 cup light corn syrup

1 teaspoon cornstarch

1/4 teaspoon baking soda

Pour milk into a 5-quart glass bowl. Microwave uncovered on 100% (high) 6 minutes or until milk boils. Stir in sugar, corn syrup, cornstarch and baking soda. Microwave on 100% (high) 20 minutes or until mixture thickens and becomes a golden brown, stirring every 5 minutes. Immediately remove from microwave; beat candy vigorously with a wooden spoon 2 minutes. Refrigerate until cool. Candy will thicken as it cools.

Each tablespoon contains:

Cal	Prot	Carb	Fib	Tot. Fat	Sat Fat	Chol	Sodium
71	1g	17g	0	0	0	1mg	25mg

   ❦   ❦   ❦

It was a common practice for people in Southern New Mexico and West Texas to shop in the mercado *or market in Ciudad Juárez. If my parents were making a trip, we would beg them to bring us our special treat. That was a small, round wooden box containing our favorite soft-caramel candy,* Cajeta. *It was fun just to eat the caramel candy right out of the wooden box. This microwave recipe for Cajeta makes a soft caramel, great when eaten by the spoonful or used as a sweet topping for ice cream.*

Pipitoria con Chile

Chile Peanut Brittle

I owe my microwave Chile Peanut Brittle recipe to my dad. He likes a little chile in everything, even for a different taste in confections.

Power level: high
Cooking time: 9 minutes
Servings: about 1 pound candy

1 cup shelled, unsalted peanuts

1/4 cup flaked coconut

1 teaspoon vegetable oil

2 teaspoons red-chile powder

1 cup sugar

1/2 cup light corn syrup

1 teaspoon margarine

1 teaspoon baking soda

❦ **Variation**
Use chopped, unsalted cashews in place of peanuts.

Combine peanuts, coconut, oil and chile powder in a glass pie plate. Microwave on 100% (high) 2 minutes, stirring after 1 minute; set aside.

Grease or spray with vegetable cooking spray a baking sheet; set aside. Combine sugar and corn syrup in a 5-quart bowl. Microwave on 100% (high) 6 minutes, stirring after 3 minutes. Stir in margarine. Microwave on 100% (high) 1 minute. Immediately stir in baking soda. Add peanut mixture; stir until light and foamy. Pour mixture onto greased baking sheet. Butter your hands or a rolling pin; flatten the candy. Let peanut brittle stand until cool; then break into pieces.

Each ounce contains:

Cal	Prot	Carb	Fib	Tot. Fat	Sat. Fat	Chol	Sodium
139	2g	22g	1g	5g	1g	0	67mg

Dulce de Coco

Coconut Candy

If you like coconut, you'll enjoy this light, creamy candy.

Power level: high
Cooking time: 26 to 27 minutes
Servings: 32 to 36 pieces

1 tablespoon vegetable oil

**3 cups flaked coconut or
1 (7-oz.) pkg. flaked coconut**

2 tablespoons margarine

1 cup granulated sugar

1/4 cup light corn syrup

3/4 cup lowfat milk

1/8 teaspoon baking soda

1/8 teaspoon salt

1 teaspoon vanilla extract

2 cups unsifted powdered sugar

Pour oil into a 9-inch glass pie plate; blend in coconut. Cover with waxed paper; microwave on 100% (high) 4 minutes, stirring at 1 minute intervals. When browned, set aside.

Grease or spray with vegetable cooking spray a baking sheet; set aside. Combine margarine, granulated sugar, corn syrup, milk, baking soda and salt in a 5-quart glass bowl.

Microwave on 100% (high) 22 to 23 minutes or until candy reaches soft-ball stage, stirring every 5 minutes. To test for soft-ball stage, drop 1/4 teaspoon hot mixture into very cold water. It should form a soft ball. If using a microwave-safe candy thermometer, mixture is ready at 235F (115C).

When candy reaches soft-ball stage, vigorously beat in coconut, vanilla and powdered sugar with a wooden spoon. Drop by teaspoonfuls onto greased baking sheet. Cool candy before serving.

Each piece contains:

Cal	Prot	Carb	Fib	Tot. Fat	Sat Fat	Chol	Sodium
88	0	16g	1g	3g	2g	0	38mg

Jamoncillo de Nuez

Vanilla Fudge with Nuts

A delicious candy with a light, creamy texture.

Power level: high
Cooking time: 11 minutes
Servings: 24 pieces

1/2 cup lowfat milk

1/4 cup margarine

1-1/2 cups granulated sugar

1/2 teaspoon salt

1/8 teaspoon baking soda

1 teaspoon vanilla extract

1-1/4 cups powdered sugar

24 pecan halves (1/3 cup pecans)

❦ **Variation**
For Jamoncillo de Chocolate, add 1/3 cup unsweetened cocoa powder and 2 tablespoons vegetable oil to lowfat milk.

Grease or spray with vegetable cooking spray a baking sheet; set aside. Combine milk, margarine and granulated sugar in a 5-quart glass bowl. Microwave on 100% (high), uncovered, 4 minutes. Stir in salt and baking soda; microwave on 100% (high), uncovered, 7 minutes or until candy reaches soft-ball stage, stirring after 4 minutes. To test for soft-ball stage, drop 1/4 teaspoon hot mixture into very cold water. It should form a soft ball. If using a microwave-safe candy thermometer, mixture is ready when temperature reaches 235F (115C).

When mixture reaches soft-ball stage, stir in vanilla and powdered sugar; beat vigorously with a wooden spoon until candy begins to thicken. Butter your hands. While candy is still hot, quickly shape into 24 balls; place on greased baking sheet. Press a pecan half into each fudge ball. Cool well before serving.

Each piece contains:

Cal	Prot	Carb	Fib	Tot. Fat	Sat Fat	Chol	Sodium
93	0	18g	0	2g	0	0	75mg

Melcocha

Anise Candy

A traditional Mexican candy with the flavor of anise (licorice).

Power level: high
Cooking time: 16 to 17 minutes
Servings: 12 pieces

1 cup (1/2 lb.) piloncillo (panocha) crumbled or dark-brown sugar

1/2 cup light corn syrup

1-1/2 teaspoons anise flavoring

2 teaspoons baking soda

To soften piloncillo, place in a small bowl. Cover with waxed paper; microwave on 100% (high) 1 to 2 minutes. Crumble with a fork.

Combine piloncillo and light corn syrup in a 5-quart bowl. Microwave, uncovered, on 100% (high) 16 to 17 minutes or until candy reaches hard-crack stage, stirring every 5 minutes. To test for hard-crack stage, drop 1/4 teaspoon mixture into very cold water. It should harden and crack. If using a microwave candy thermometer, mixture is ready at 300F (150C).

When mixture reaches hard-crack stage, immediately add anise flavoring and baking soda. Beat vigorously with a wooden spoon until light and foamy. Pour into 12 mounds on greased baking sheet.

Butter your hands; roll each mound into a long stick. Twist to form a rope-like stick. Place sticks on greased baking sheet; let cool. Candy is ready when it hardens.

Each piece contains:

Cal	Prot	Carb	Fib	Tot. Fat	Sat. Fat	Chol	Sodium
106	0	28g	0	0	0	0	151mg

Pastelitos de Boda

Bride's Cookies

A traditional cookie served for special occasions— especially weddings and holidays.

Power level: medium-high
Cooking time: 6 to 7 minutes
Servings: about 42 cookies

2 cups all-purpose flour

3/4 cup powdered sugar

1-1/2 teaspoons vanilla extract

3/4 cup margarine

2 to 3 tablespoons water

1 cup chopped pecans or pecan pieces

3/4 cup powdered sugar

Grease or line with waxed paper a 12" x 8" flat-bottom casserole; set aside. Combine flour, 3/4 cup powdered sugar, vanilla and margarine in a bowl. Blend with an electric mixer; gradually add 2 to 3 tablespoons water, as needed, to make a soft dough. Stir in pecans.

Shape into 1-inch balls. Place 12 balls, evenly spaced, in casserole.

Place casserole in microwave on top of an inverted glass bowl for uniform baking. Microwave on 70% (medium-high) 6 to 7 minutes, turning dish after 3 minutes. Cookies are done when a wooden pick inserted in center comes out clean. Roll cookies in remaining 3/4 cup powdered sugar. Cool on a rack. Repeat baking process with remaining dough.

Each cookie contains:

Cal	Prot	Carb	Fib	Tot. Fat	Sat Fat	Chol	Sodium
76	1g	9g	0	4g	1g	0	40mg

Bizcochitos

Anise Cookies

Combining wine or orange juice with anise gives these crispy cookies a unique flavor.

Power level: medium-high
Cooking time: 6 to 7 minutes
Servings: 30 to 32 cookies

1/2 cup vegetable oil

1/2 cup sugar

1 egg

2 teaspoons anise seeds, crushed, or anise flavoring

2 cups all-purpose flour

1/2 teaspoon baking powder

1/2 teaspoon salt

3 tablespoons wine or orange juice

1/2 cup sugar

1 teaspoon ground cinnamon

In a large mixer bowl cream oil, 1/2 cup sugar, egg and anise seeds or flavoring until mixture is light and fluffy. Set aside.

Combine flour, baking powder and salt; gradually add to creamed mixture with wine or juice. Beat until a soft dough forms. Combine 1/2 cup sugar and cinnamon; set aside.

Grease or line with waxed paper a 12" x 8" flat-bottom casserole. Shape dough into 1-inch balls. Place 12 balls, evenly spaced, in casserole. Flatten balls with a glass bottom until dough is 1/4-inch thick.

Place casserole in microwave on top of an inverted glass bowl for uniform baking. Microwave on 70% (medium-high) 6 to 7 minutes, turning dish after 3 minutes.

Remove immediately, dip cookies in sugar mixture; cool on a rack. Repeat for remaining cookies.

Each cookie contains:

Cal	Prot	Carb	Fib	Tot. Fat	Sat Fat	Chol	Sodium
86	1g	12g	0	4g	0	7mg	41mg

Mexican Cocoa

A delicious hot drink.

Power level: high
Cooking time: 3 to 4 minutes
Servings: 4 cups

**2 (1-oz.) squares semisweet
  chocolate**

4 cups lowfat milk

2 tablespoons sugar

1/4 teaspoon ground cinnamon

1/8 teaspoon ground nutmeg

Pinch of salt

Combine all ingredients in a 4-cup glass measuring cup. Microwave on 100% (high) 3 to 4 minutes until hot and chocolate is melted. Blend with a whisk. Serve hot.

Each cup contains:

Cal	Prot	Carb	Fib	Tot. Fat	Sat Fat	Chol	Sodium
199	9g	26g	0	8g	5g	10mg	125mg

🐛   🐛   🐛

The only variety store in our neighborhood was my great-aunt Lupe's tienda. She sold sundries, including a large assortment of penny candy. On her candy counter was a large jar filled with Bizcochitos *or anise cookies. Every Saturday she would have Doña Lucia, an elderly friend, come and bake Bizcochitos for the store. I never hesitated at the chance to lend a hand. My job was to dip the freshly baked thin cookies into the sugar mixture. I enjoyed doing this because I could easily sneak a Bizcochito when I thought no one was looking. Without fail, Bizcochitos and Pastelitos de Bodas were served at birthday parties, baptisms, weddings and other social occasions. Enjoy them with a cup of Mexican Cocoa.*

Lupe's Champurrado

Lupe's Chocolate Corn Drink

My great-aunt Lupe's recipe for Champurrado.

Power level: high, medium-high
Cooking time: 10 minutes
Servings: about 3 cups

2-1/2 cups water

2 (3-inch) cinnamon sticks

3 tablespoons masa harina

5 tablespoons sugar

3 tablespoons unsweetened cocoa powder or 1 (1-oz.) square unsweetened chocolate

1/4 teaspoon anise flavoring

1/2 cup whipping cream

Whipped cream, if desired

❧   ❧   ❧

Corn drinks have always been popular in Mexico. My mother's favorite was Champurrado. *It's flavored with cinnamon and anise. Although masa harina is included, this is a light drink.*

Place water and cinnamon sticks in a 2-quart glass bowl. Cover with waxed paper; microwave on 100% (high) 5 minutes or until water begins to boil. Let stand 5 minutes. Strain cinnamon-flavored water into a 2-quart measuring cup; discard cinnamon sticks. Add masa harina, sugar and cocoa or chocolate to cinnamon water; beat with a whisk until well blended.

Cover measuring cup with waxed paper; microwave on 70% (medium-high) 5 minutes, stirring after 2-1/2 minutes. Add anise flavoring and 1/2 cup whipping cream; beat with electric mixer at medium speed 1 minute. Pour mixture into cups or mugs for serving. Top with whipped cream, if desired. A cinnamon stick can be added for a swizzle.

Each cup contains:

Cal	Prot	Carb	Fib	Tot. Fat	Sat. Fat	Chol	Sodium
237	2g	30g	3g	14g	8g	44mg	16mg

Café Mexicano

Mexican Coffee

An excellent beverage for breakfast or after an evening meal.

Power level: high
Cooking time: 5 minutes
Servings: 2 cups

2 cups water

2 tablespoons piloncillo (panocha) or dark-brown sugar

2 (3-inch) cinnamon sticks

2 whole cloves

1 tablespoon instant-coffee powder

Milk or cream, if desired

Combine water, piloncillo or brown sugar, cinnamon sticks and cloves in a 2-quart measuring cup. Microwave on 100% (high) 5 minutes or until water begins to boil. Let stand 3 minutes; then stir. Strain mixture into another glass container, discarding cinnamon and cloves. Stir in coffee powder. Pour into cups or mugs. Serve with milk or cream, if desired.

Each cup contains:

Cal	Prot	Carb	Fib	Tot. Fat	Sat. Fat	Chol	Sodium
53	0	14g	0	0	0	0	14mg

Agua Fresca de Tamarindo

Tamarind Cooler

Tamarind is an elongated brown pod. The pulp, when extracted and mixed with sugar and water, makes a pleasant drink with a bit of a tropical tang.

Power level: high
Cooking time: 10 minutes
Servings: 4 glasses

1/4 pound (4 oz.) tamarind pods (about 6 pods)

5 cups water

3/4 cups sugar

1 tablespoon lime juice

Wash tamarind pods and soften by putting pods in a 2-quart bowl, add 5 cups water. Cover with waxed paper and microwave on 100% (high) 10 minutes or until water boils. Strain pods reserving liquid. Run pods under water to cool. Remove skin and strings from pods and scrape fruit pulp from seeds.

Place pulp along with 2 cups reserved tamarind water and sugar in blender and blend 45 to 60 seconds or until well blended. Add to remaining 2 cups reserved water. Add lime juice and refrigerate at least 1 hour before serving. When ready to serve, pour into glasses over ice, if desired.

Each 8 oz. glass contains:

Cal	Prot	Carb	Fib	Tot. Fat	Sat. Fat	Chol	Sodium
213	1g	55g	2g	0	0	0	9mg

Horchata de Arroz

Rice Drink

This popular Mexican drink is made from steeped rice and toasted almonds. Horchatas can also be made with melon seeds or other varieties of nuts. Blending and straining the rice and almonds after steeping gives a smooth, pleasant-tasting drink.

Power level: high
Cooking time: 11 to 12 minutes
Servings: 4 cups

2 tablespoons white long-grain rice

2 tablespoons toasted, slivered almonds

4 cups water

1/4 cup sugar

2 (3-inch) cinnamon sticks

Rinse rice. Put rice in a 2-quart measuring cup or bowl, add almonds, water, sugar and cinnamon sticks. Microwave on 100% (high) 11 to 12 minutes or until water begins to boil. Cover and set aside 30 minutes.

Discard cinnamon sticks. Pour mixture in blender. Process about 2 minutes until rice and almonds are blended. Refrigerate 1 hour before serving. Strain and pour into glasses over ice, if desired.

Each cup contains:

Cal	Prot	Carb	Fib	Tot. Fat	Sat. Fat	Chol	Sodium
94	1g	18g	1g	2g	0	0	1mg

❧ **Variation**

Horchata de Arroz con Fresas
Strawberry Rice Drink

Increase sugar to 1/2 cup and omit cinnamon sticks. After straining horchata, add 2 cups sliced fresh or frozen strawberries. Place strawberries in blender with 2 cups prepared horchata and blend thoroughly, about 1 minute. Add blended strawberries to remaining horchata, stir. When ready to serve, pour into glasses over ice.

Horchata de Arroz con Piña
Pineapple Rice Drink

Increase sugar to 1/2 cup. After straining horchata, add 2 cups fresh pineapple, cut into chunks or 1 (20-oz.) can pineapple chunks, drained. Place pineapple in blender with 2 cups prepared horchata. Blend thoroughly, about 45 to 60 seconds. Add blended pineapple mixture to remaining horchata and stir. When ready to serve, pour into glasses over ice.

Horchata de Arroz de Chocolate
Chocolate Rice Drink

Add 1 cup skim milk, 3 tablespoons nonfat dry milk powder and 1 to 2 tablespoons chocolate syrup or chocolate milk powder mix and stir well. Makes 2 cups.

For a hot chocolate drink heat 1 cup Horchata de Chocolate in a cup and microwave on 100% (high) 2 minutes or until hot. ¡Delicioso!

Aguas Frescas

Fresh Fruit Drinks

A refreshing summer drink.

Power level: high
Cooking time: 5 minutes
Servings: 6 cups

4 cups water

1/3 cup sugar

3 cups fresh or frozen strawberries, or cantaloupe, or watermelon chunks, or pineapple

1 cup ice cubes

In a glass bowl combine water and sugar. Microwave uncovered on 100% (high) 5 minutes or until sugar dissolves. Stir well and allow to cool in the refrigerator about 1 hour.

In a mixer bowl combine 2 cups sugar-sweetened water, strawberries or other fruit and ice and beat until well blended.

Add remaining 2 cups sugar-sweetened water, stir and refrigerate at least 1 hour before serving. When ready to serve, pour into glasses over ice, if desired.

Each cup contains:

Cal	Prot	Carb	Fib	Tot. Fat	Sat. Fat	Chol	Sodium
65	0	16g	2g	0	0	0	1mg

Index